Lists That Saved My Life

ANGEL

TUCCY

ALSO BY ANGEL TUCCY

Lists That Saved My Business

Sex, Drugs & Rock N Roll
3 Keys to a Healthier Lifestyle

Sex, Drugs & Rock N Roll
90 Day Companion Journal

SUPER-Marketing
Audio Seminar

Experience Pros University Workbook

Dedicated to my children, Alycia, Lauren and Michael
May you have wings and roots.

TABLE OF CONTENTS

Lists That Saved My Life

FOREWORD

They say that every once in a very great while, something special... something "magical" comes along... and changes *EVERYTHING*. I am of the firm conviction that just such a time happened the very moment that you picked up this book!

One might be tempted to categorize this book as a work of fiction, given the fact that it is the story of a woman who claims to balance life as a full-time wife, a full-time mother, and a full-time entrepreneur with a thriving consulting business, a growing "University" of business development, and a very successful radio show. May I encourage you to resist that temptation? I bear witness to the very reality – unbelievable as it may seem – of the world according to Angel.

Perhaps even more importantly, I am the recipient of many of the benefits that Angel's world has to offer us – all of us – who invest the time to not only read – but to put into practice the practical words of wisdom found within these pages.

There was a time, many years ago, that I would tease Angel by making reference to her "Franklin Planner World". It always seemed to conflict with my much more "creative" methodology of flying by the seat of my pants. Today, however, I can honestly tell you that I not only embrace Angel's Franklin Planner World... I have come to rely upon it each and every day. It is a source of comfort... a source of organization... a source of energy turned into action in my own world. And it can be the same for you!

I used to stand on the philosophy that "people don't change". Today I am a living, breathing testimony that people DO change when they are appropriately motivated by truth, simplicity and a sense of purpose. You will find all of those qualities in the words of this book. You will find the heart of my business partner... my friend. And who knows? You just might find yourself... changing!

Welcome to the revolutionary world... of Angel!

By Eric S. Reamer, co-owner of Experience Pros, LLC; co-founder of Experience Pros University and co-host of The Experience Pros Radio Show

PROLOGUE

We were driving back from a camping trip and I was sitting in the passenger seat watching the traffic go by. The kids were in the back seat reading books and it was pretty quiet, all except for the white noise that was coming from the engine. I don't even think the radio was on. We were all tired from the trip and anxious to get home, but we were still two hours away.

I started thinking about what I needed to do once we were home. I was recalling all the things we had forgotten in our haste to get out of town on the spur-of-the-moment. We have a friend who rents out campers and this one wasn't being used this weekend. Since the kids had a three-day weekend from school, we accepted the last-minute offer to take it. On Friday morning, we threw everything we could think we would need into the camper and stopped at the grocery store on the way out of town.

Among a few other things, we had forgotten to bring firewood, an axe, or anything to make a campfire with, so that made roasting marshmallows quite interesting. One thing that is consistently true about our family is that whenever we travel together it is always a comical adventure. Thank goodness we aren't on a reality television show. The whole world would be laughing at us as we haphazardly attempted to bring a lit scrolled-up paper plate from the camper to the fire pit. We had gathered up pinecones and built a pyramid of garbage to light on fire. It took three attempts as the kids lined up to create a wind barrier. Our attempts were a success and we roasted a full bag of marshmallows. The next day, we were able to buy firewood from the campground host.

You'll probably be able to discern for yourself that I'm more of an 'indoor' gal, but every year, I make the effort to be the outdoorsy type for my family's sake. It's a tradition to take my father camping every year for Father's Day, but I've never quite mastered it. Please forgive me if I seem ill prepared for the necessary needs of living in nature for a few days. My family really has tried to convert me. My contribution is that my camping antics make for great family stories during the holidays.

Back in the camper, I started creating a mental checklist in my head. Then my mind wandered onto something else and eventually landed on the book ideas that I have been toying around with. I really want to write. I have been thinking of writing a book for too long now. It's about time to make a decision on a topic and just get it done. I've had several conversations with other friends who have published their literary works and they've all been very encouraging to me. The bottom line is I just need to do it.

"Go and write your book," they tell me.

I thought of a conversation I had the week before with someone I had just met a few weeks ago. I thought of the lists of things that had to be done. I thought of the book that I wanted to write.

Slowly, the thoughts all blurred together and I shouted out, "I'm going to write a book about lists that saved my life!"

Right there in the camper, on the way back from a three-day camping trip, I pitched my book idea to my favorite budding authors, my three children.

All were in unison when they said "that's a great idea, mom!" and we started brainstorming about the chapter titles.

We quickly came up with the ten lists that I regularly use and then settled back down. It returned back to being quiet, while I started dreaming about this book.

6

CHAPTER 1
My Secret Life of Lists

If you don't care where you're going,
it doesn't much matter what route you take. –Winnie the Pooh

A week before this book became a sparkle in my eye, I had met with a working mom who was just starting her own entrepreneurial career.

"I want to pick your brain", she said to me, "I want to know how you balance your job and your family and keep it all together."

When she asked me that question, I thought to myself, isn't that the question that all working moms ask? Whenever I talk with other women, mothers in particular, but women in general, it seems as if we are in a constant struggle to keep it all flowing and still look like the *En Jolie* woman at the end of the day. That perfume commercial told women that we could work all day long, come home and take care of the house and still be very sexy at the end of the day.

I tell everyone that I am a stay-at-home mom, even though I work a full-time job. That's my daily internal struggle. I desperately want to be the best mom for my children, but at the same time, I have goals and talents that I personally want to pursue for me.

If I pursue my own dreams, without sacrificing my family, then I get to be the best "me" and in turn, they get to have the best mom. My dreams and goals give me life and feed my soul in a different way than my family does. When I am motivated and energized, all of a sudden, I am also a wealth of wisdom and creativity.

They say that if you want something to get done, you should give it to a busy person and most days, I believe that. My mom was like that, too. I share a lot of her drive and her mannerisms. She never makes excuses. She never stops moving. There are days where I am juggling so many things that I amaze even myself at how much I can accomplish. Even though I need a day of rest just as much as the next person, when I don't have something to strive towards, I end up moving through my day pretty much like a zombie. I can get really fast at those Sudoku puzzles and spider solitaire on my computer, but at the end of the week, is that the legacy I'm shooting for?

My family is my legacy – but I am so much more than my kid's mom. I feel like there is so much more that I am meant to do – and not only tasks, chores and errands, I want to live a life. I want to live a full life. I want a life full of relationships, good health and confident children. I don't mean confident in a way that describes sacrificing everything you love to accomplish a goal, but confident in the terms of loving, giving love, feeling loved and sleeping well at the end of the day because you went forward in the direction of your dreams. I pray that my children dream.

My current situation consists of co-owning my own consulting business with a very patient and understanding business partner, Eric. Eric took me under his wing and taught me everything he knows about running a business. He was the first person to convince me I could speak in front of an audience. I had to memorize all of my material when I first started speaking because my hand would shake too much to hold onto my notes. I was a nervous wreck, but he swore to me that I was good at it. Eventually, I got used to it and even now, I rarely admit it out loud to him, but I like it.

Being an entrepreneur keeps me running during the week. My home, husband and family keep me running simultaneously. My husband is also an entrepreneur. That means that we both work on one hundred percent commissions. If our businesses don't make money, neither do we. We pay for our own health insurance and fund our own retirement accounts. We don't have a base salary to keep us afloat if we decide to go on vacation or take time off for sick children. We are self-sufficient because we have to be.

I am a mother of twin teen daughters and one pre-teen son. My husband and I attend all of the plays, band concerts and football games that our children perform in. Most of the time, their grandparents attend, too. Most of our immediate family lives in the same county as we do. It makes for fun and loud family get-togethers. The stories we share get more and more embellished each year. And funnier, too.

Each week, my husband and I go on a date. Granted, it's to the grocery store, but it's a date. Don't scoff yet. It works for us.

We stop and grab a latte and then we stroll through the aisles for one-hour without children in tow. Did you hear that? We get one full hour every week without the distraction of children. Now that our kids are a little older, we can do this guilt-free! And trust me; the mommy-guilt is real. It can be paralyzing and frustrating and depressing. I am in favor of anytime I can do something that eliminates the mommy-guilt altogether. If I can help another mommy overcome the invisible wall of guilt, then we both feel like Super Woman for a day.

I am a sister, a friend and a Dave Ramsey 'Financial Peace' fanatic. I love to stay fit – and most weekends, when the kids aren't catching up on homework, we love to take an afternoon and go for a bike ride or a hike together. We live in glorious Colorado weather where we can play outdoors three hundred days a year. It makes it a little easier to stay active when the fresh outdoors are so accessible.

So when my new acquaintance asked me how I keep it all balanced, I gave her my secret that has helped me stay organized for years; I am a list-maker. It's not sexy, it's not innovative, but it works. I have a list for everything and everything starts as a list. In my own world, my lists have saved my sanity. I don't have to remember everything, though I have a knack for holding onto miscellaneous information long after it's needed. I think I get that from my mom. My lists keep me organized, on time and current with birthdays. One of my lists helped my family of five go to Europe for five weeks with only five outfits – true story!

I'm a Franklin Planner lover and the Franklin system teaches you to prioritize your task lists on a daily basis. Benjamin Franklin was a list lover, too. In fact, he never went any where without his little black book of lists. His theory was that he didn't need to remember every thing; he only needed to remember where he wrote it down. Benjamin Franklin accomplished so much every single day – and has a legacy for organization that has stood the test of time. To me, the electronic age and paperless world we live in makes the lists even more necessary. The Internet and the computer are designed to keep us running so efficiently, that now I have lists in the cyber world, too. And can I please take this moment to remind you to back up your data? For those of you who have this task automated, it's a good idea to double-check on those automated systems.

I have a girlfriend who lost a year's worth of files because her automated system wasn't backing up correctly. When my computer crashed last year and Eric broke the news to me that nothing was retrievable, I cried. I felt as if a wave kept crashing over me every time I remembered something else that I would never see again. Photos: crash! Files: gone! Accounting: irretrievable! Memos: missing! Research, articles, stories, proposals, invoices and receipts: all lost forever. It was an emotional disaster. Everything had to be recreated or accepted as items that would forever be lost. Please, please, back up your data.

Backing up our data is one of those new priorities that have made its way into our regular routines. This wasn't a task we had to do a few years ago. With so many new changes being thrown at us, how do we decide what things are important and what things can slide for a while? I had just had one of those talks with my daughters, Alycia and Lauren, about their grades and making homework a priority. It was one of those conversations that I will remember for a long time – not just because of what I said to my girls, but how valid the lesson is, even for me.

We talked about the conflict between emotion and logic. We talked about how it's easy to look at the things that need to be done, such as homework. But even if it weighs in heavy on the balance scales as the right thing to do, we still struggle with doing it. The thing we want to do, such as socializing and recreational activities, always wins out over the thing we need to do. Emotion wins over logic every time. The secret lies in matching our dreams up to motivate us to do the things we don't want to do. For example, a B-average student gets better insurance rates, so getting a driver's license could be a great motivator to improve their school grades. No B's, No Keys! It's like dangling a carrot in front of a horse to get it to move.

Years ago, I heard about an example of a pickle jar that taught me how to keep my priorities straight. Mark Twain said, "People don't fail because they want to fail; they fail because they don't know how to succeed". This example helped me to create a word picture in my mind for prioritizing my task list. Often, just knowing 'how' can set me back on the right path for success.

Imagine a large pickle jar sitting empty on your counter. Surrounding the pickle jar are rocks of varying sizes. There are large rocks, medium sized-rocks, small rocks, gravel, sand and a jug of water. If you were asked to fill that jar with all the items on the counter, how would you go about it? If you start with the sand, then add the small and medium-sized rocks, you'd discover that the large rocks would not fit. However, if you put the large rocks into the jar first, you'll discover that the small and medium-sized rocks would slide into place, filling the empty spaces around the large rocks. The gravel and sand would then fill in the remaining crevices and there would even be enough room to hold the jug of water.

Prioritizing our tasks is a lot like filling an empty pickle jar. Each day, we start with an empty jar and it's up to us to fill the jar with what is important, in other words; the large rocks. I've discovered two things that really help me find balance in choosing how to spend my time. First, it turns out that there aren't that many large rocks. Most of my day is full of sand and gravel-like items. These are things like doing laundry, checking emails, reading through Facebook posts, running errands or organizing my business cards. Granted, all of these tasks need to get done sometime throughout the week, but I find that if I start with the small-rock items, then I never have time for the big rocks; my family, my health, my friendships, my customers, my personal time.

The second thing that really helps me out, mostly in diverting any of that mommy-guilt that I could harbor, is that my life doesn't have to be balanced every single day. When I think of the teeter-totter on the playground, it's fascinating when the two ends are balanced in mid-air. But the real fun happens when there is motion in the seesaw. Real energy comes from the challenge of trying to keep the seesaw in balance. There may be some days that I work fourteen hours, but on the flip side, there are days that I don't start work until after 10:00 a.m.

I have Saturdays where I lounge in front of the Wii with my kids all day long. There are many days that I get to sit with my feet up and listen as my son reads to me out loud, which I absolutely love. One of my favorite times of the day comes at the very end where I spend time talking to and tucking in my girls before we all fall asleep.

14

When I took my babies to the pediatrician because I was concerned that they weren't eating enough, she consoled this young mother by telling me that all children will eat when they were hungry if given the chance. She told me not to worry if one day they seemed to eat very little because over the course of the week, they would consume all the nutrition they needed.

That advice from my pediatrician has helped me tremendously. I told my new friend, each day doesn't have to look balanced, because by the end of the week, it all teeters out.

CHAPTER TWO
The Ultimate List – My Calendar

Lost time is never found. – Benjamin Franklin

Jay and I were sitting at lunch and something about the conversation triggered a thought for me. We were talking about Michael's play rehearsals and I remembered that my sister-in-law had invited us to see our niece's play performance. My niece was performing in a play the coming weekend. I told my husband to call his sister and let her know we would be attending our niece's play during the Saturday matinee. Unfortunately, our calendar was already booked for the two evening performances, but we all really wanted to see my niece's first performance.

We decided that the best plan was to squeeze it in on Saturday and skip the bike outing we were planning. Jay sent his sister a text message. In only a few minutes, his phone rang and it was Suzy. "You missed the play. It was last weekend." Ugh. How could that have happened? We were immediately bummed that we missed it because going to see family performances is one of our favorite things to do. Our large family takes up quite a bit of the seating in the audience and we cheer and clap the loudest.

Our emotional downfall was our own fault because when we originally found out about it, we didn't write the date into the calendar. So now, a week later, when I finally remembered, the event had already passed and we had missed it.

I believe in keeping one master calendar for everything. Rather than one calendar at home on the fridge, one on my computer at work and one in my purse or on my phone, I still carry around a Franklin binder. It's not electronic; it still requires a pen. And my pen has a fine tip and purple ink. This pen's only purpose is to write in my planner and nothing else. There is a little mailbox store in the near shopping center that carries it and if they ever stop, well, I guess I'll have to find a new pen to use! Flexibility is another great quality to being organized – and one quality I am constantly struggling with and still trying to teach to my son. I'm not always where I want to be, but I'm better than I used to be.

I love buying a new re-fill for my calendar every year and replacing my scribbled, rough-edged pages with clean, blank new sheets of pretty paper. I use different colored highlighters and symbols to keep me organized and January 1st is one of my favorite days of the year. Okay, that may be pushing it, but I really do enjoy filling my new calendar. The calendar is really my ultimate list.

I remember when I splurged and bought my first Franklin binder. Up until then, I had only spent a few dollars on a calendar, but I felt like a true businesswoman carrying around my leather Franklin planner. I met my girlfriend from high school and I was showing her all the features as if it was a brand new car. Her address was one of the first entries in the address book. I was writing down her zip code and I messed it up and had to cross it out and re-write it. I was bummed. She laughed at me and said, "Aw, don't you hate it when you want it to be all pretty and now it's scribbled?!" I realized right then that my calendar isn't a work of art, but a tool that will keep me organized. And the better the tool, the more 'used' it will look.

I don't commit to anything until I've consulted my calendar. When I read through emails and sort through the mail, I do it with my calendar at hand. I write down the parent-teacher conferences right then and I highlight the dates when the kids are off from school. Since I have had to deal with two different school schedules for all but two years, I give my son, who is on a year-round schedule, the green highlighter and my daughters get the purple highlighter. At a glance, I can determine when my kids are home from school and when I can schedule the entire day for clients because the kids are in school.

One day this summer, Lauren and Alycia wanted to go to a birthday party. They had slept in until 10:30 or so and came into my home office to ask if they could go to the party. The party was starting in less than an hour. They were supposed to meet their friends at the movie theater. In less than one hour, I needed to finish what I was working on and get it emailed over to my office for approval, secure a birthday gift, get my hands on some cash and drop the girls off at the theater. It was not going to happen.

Since then, the kids have learned to tell me about birthday parties or events that they want to go to, in advance. I don't need a lot of warning, but that summer morning, they learned the hard way that when they schedule something with their friends and it's not on mom's calendar, they have to cancel. They still rely on me for transportation, so mom's calendar is the rule. It was a tough lesson, but in the long run, I don't have to chase them for their schedule as often. It's not perfect. It was a "lesson" in communication, not a hard-fast behavioral change. As a mom, I have to focus on progress, not perfection.

Each week, my husband and I coordinate our calendars. We compare orthodontist appointments, special dates and the taxi schedule. There are many days when we have to divide and conquer to make it all happen and coordinating our calendars keeps everyone where they have to be and on-time.

Even when it's just Eric and me in the office, we still hold a weekly staff meeting to coordinate our calendar. I've learned that it's important to establish systems and protocol, even as a baby-business. Someday, we could be a huge organization and we will rely on these early habits to set our stage for success.

In fourth grade, the school curriculum includes a homework planner for each student. We encourage our kids to use their planner everyday, not only for school assignments but for their extra-curricular activities, too. They write down their doctor's appointments and friend's birthdays and each week I ask to see them. If they quickly flash it in front of me, I know it's not being used. They believe that I have that parental sixth sense and their shoulders melt when I ask them to show me what they've checked off. They would prefer to skip the planner reviews – but they would also prefer to skip doing homework, so it's not really a choice.

Jay and I try to include the kids in on our weekly calendar meetings – at least for the first few minutes. I want them to see that life doesn't have to happen *to* them. I want to teach them how to plan ahead for the mounting chaos called life. I was in high school when I fell in love with calendars – and I have many friends who don't use them. I've seen the other side and this is one of those childhood lessons my kids will use forever, just like how to properly floss their teeth. These aren't the types of things that come naturally – they have to be taught. When they are included in our calendar meeting, they have a heads up to how the week will work out. One of them might have to be dropped off a little early, or wait a little bit for a pick up, but they understand and are prepared for it. That seems to be comforting for all of us.

Besides being the ultimate list, my calendar works as a journal for me, too. I keep track of client appointments, birthdays, sales, meetings, everything all in one place. One time, my husband scoffed at me because I was filling in previous days on my calendar. Since the date had passed, he thought it was odd that I was writing in more items. He thought I did it because I wanted my calendar to look busy. I explained to him that I do this so I can keep track of the last time I had my nails done or spent the day with my mom. It works out really well when I'm reconciling my credit card statement and there's an item I don't recognize. I can refer back to my calendar and see that I went out to lunch with my girlfriend that day and the purchase makes sense when I compare it to my calendar.

When I add appointments to my calendar, I have my filtration process that I automatically go through. I don't know when I picked up this terrific tidbit, but I've learned not to commit to anything on the spot. I don't let others rush me into giving an immediate answer, even if they tell me it's urgent. I love the saying "your failure to plan does not constitute an emergency on my part". I always let people know that I'll have to check my calendar and get back to them. This buys me some time to make sure my priorities are in order and it gives me a slight edge in negotiations. Often, people will back down on their requests or throw in something special if they think it will gain them extra favor with my calendar. I don't intentionally use it as a negotiation tactic, but I have seen it work in my favor on more than one occasion.

If I don't want to do something or it conflicts with another event, I have learned to say, "I'm sorry, but I have another appointment/event at the same time. I'll have to miss your event or reschedule for another time." This has been a saving grace for me, more than once. No more getting caught without an answer, no more avoiding the neighbor who keeps inviting me to her "let's drink cocktails and complain about the men in our life" party. I simply have another engagement and it's unfortunate that I'll have to miss. My calendar helps me to say "no", and if necessary, my calendar is the bad guy; "I'm sorry, I can't see you that day, my calendar won't let me."

One of the reasons that I adore the gal who cuts my hair is that she is great at her job. She is fabulous with a pair of scissors. The other reason is that I can reserve my next two haircuts and I have appointments scheduled up to fourteen weeks in advance. I've been going to her for over ten years and I love that I can schedule her in and then not worry about it. I can tell by the length of my bangs when it's time for a new cut and when I look at my calendar, I see that it's scheduled for the same week!

When I schedule a meeting with clients, I schedule around my children. Sometimes, the conflict in my calendar is that I want to be home when my children arrive home from school in the afternoon. This has continued to grow in importance to me as my children have gotten older. I want to be available when they want to talk. My friend calls it 'being present'.

I try to plan my day to be home between the hours of 3:00 and 5:00 p.m. Does that mean that sometimes I go back to work? Absolutely. But I discovered that I have a window of opportunity with my children. The window of opportunity is slim and occurs when they first arrive home from school. As soon as they walk in the door from school, they are famished and they scour the fridge and the pantry for a snack. During that time, it might be thirty minutes or so, they are so chatty. They are wired for sound and they talk and they talk. They tell me about their day, about their friends, about their teachers. If I miss this window and ask them later at the dinner table about their day, the response is: "fine". So I make it a point to "calendar" my appointments around this time. Does it always work? No, but throughout the week, it all teeters out.

I calendar my priorities (my big rocks) first. This means that client meetings, lunch with a girlfriend, a yoga class or a trip to the nail salon gets put in first and then my filing, checkbook balancing and laundry and errands happen around those things.

I have several quick tips and symbols that help me to look at my calendar and see at-a-glance what I have coming up. I use the happy face symbol to remind me of birthdays. When my husband still worked for a company, I used the dollar sign to remind me of paydays. Now, I use the dollar sign to remind me to pay bills. As a consultant, I'm often asked to speak for groups. I highlight all my speaking events in yellow so I can keep track of how to prepare for the week. The school schedule is highlighted and everything else gets written in on a first-come, first-served basis. And, if it's not on the calendar, frankly, it doesn't happen.

Calendar Symbols

$	Payday or Pay Bills
☺	Birthday or Anniversary
@	Meeting with
#	Phone Call

CHAPTER THREE
The What-To-Do List

The difference between try and triumph
is a little umph, - Unknown

Each week starts out with a fresh list of things to-do. It doesn't seem to matter how much I accomplished the week before, there is always a new list of things I'd like to get done. For example, this week, I need to schedule eye appointments for all three children, Alycia and Lauren need haircuts, I need to write a marketing schedule for a client, meet with my radio producer, pull my annual credit report and pay bills for both my household and my business.

While the To-Do list is never-ending, it is the one tool that helps me accomplish so much. Without it, too many items would be left to chance and I would find myself reacting to every situation rather than being proactive and being ahead of the game. With my To-Do list in hand, I can be prepared in advance and it reduces those panic attacks that happen when I realize that something was forgotten.

I keep a pad in my nightstand, next to the bed. I call it my 'Oh, Shoot!' pad, named after my golf tournament days. When I was preparing for my first tournament, someone handed me a little three-inch by five-inch spiral bound notebook. She told me not go anywhere with out it.

"Keep it with you at all times", she emphasized, "even in the bathroom!"

The 'Oh, Shoot' pad got a lot of use that summer. I would be out walking on the course and suddenly remember something that I needed to do once I got back to my desk. Or I would run into someone and I would use the pad to write down messages or phone numbers. Mostly, I would need it once I got home and inevitably recalled something important and I would write it into my "Oh, Shoot!' pad.

Now, I keep a pad next to my bed and as I'm falling asleep, or remember an item first thing in the morning – I write it into my 'Oh, Shoot' pad. My husband keeps one, too.

My brain does a lot of its best work while there's white noise going on. A lot of my ideas and details get worked out while I'm blow-drying my hair or riding in the car. I often grab the pad from the bedside table and bring it into the bathroom with me. I'll have to turn the dryer off, make a few notes and go back to styling my hair. Some of my best seminar ideas have come from being under the heat. Eric and I conduct most of our consultations on-site, so that means that we spend a lot of time in the car driving to and from appointments. We work out most of our talking points while we're in the car. I've dubbed the car the 'think tank'. Even at the gym, I don't listen to music or wear headphones. I listen to my brain. I can work out a lot of details while simultaneously working on my heart rate. I once had someone mention this to me at our recreation center.

He noticed that I seemed to be watching the televisions ahead of the elliptical machines, but I wasn't listening.

"Isn't it hard to workout with out a headset?" he asked.

Every one I know takes their iPods to the gym. I was even given one as a gift that included a nifty armband. I do like the music that's on my iPod and once in a while, I'll listen to it, but mostly, I prefer to listen to the voices in my head. It's very productive for me as long as I keep a notepad close by to jot down my thoughts.

There are two ways that I use my To-Do list. One way I use it is to keep a running tab for the week. When I have a few spare moments, I look at the list and see what I can get done in that amount of time. If I have ten minutes, I can call the optometrist and schedule those appointments. I can email the producer to set up a time to meet. For the items that take more time, I use the To-Do list to create my schedule for the week. I calendar the client marketing schedule for Tuesday afternoon and paying bills on Wednesday morning.

By scheduling the 'big stuff', the small stuff finds its way into my cracks of time. I may be home twenty minutes before the kids arrive so I'll listen to the voicemail, fold a load of laundry, feed the fish and water the plants. In the morning before I leave for work, I'll throw a load of laundry in and empty the dishwasher. I'll leave a book in my computer bag for research while I'm waiting for appointments. When I make use of my down time, I am more efficient – and I find that I have plenty of down time in my day. There's way more down time, it seems, than productive time. I'm not sure why that is, but between traffic, long lines, being put on hold and waiting for appointments to start, all my sand and pea-gravel-type items make their way into getting done.

My friend, Rachel gave me great advice for the never-ending dirty dishes issue we had at our house. I was complaining about the countertop always having dirty dishes on it. We would run the dishwasher every few days or so, but in the meantime, we would stack the dishes on the countertop and I hated the way it looked. I didn't know how to get away from it. Now, we run the dishwasher every night and empty it every morning. With this new method, I never have the stacks of dirty dishes hanging out on the counters or in the sink. Now, as the dishes get used, they go straight into the emptied dishwasher. The dishwasher is always ready for dirty dishes and the countertop stays clear. With the low-water usage of most dishwashers these days, this is really economical and keeps everyone from trying to guess whether or not the dishwasher has been run. No matter what, we run it every night and we empty it every morning. Because we have a family of five, this is necessary anyway. Only now it's scheduled and we don't have to make a decision on whether or not the dishwasher is full enough to press start.

When I grew up, we owned a dishwasher in my latter years of living at home, but we were never allowed to use it because my parents felt like it was a waste of water. And very few items were allowed to go into the dishwasher. My mom preferred that one of us kids hand wash, so I brought that emotional baggage into my home. Thank goodness for friends who will give you housekeeping advice that works. Thanks, Rachel.

We also used to struggle with "who has to empty it?" but not anymore. We timed the event and discovered that it takes three to five minutes to empty the dishwasher, so whoever uses the first dishes in the morning (usually my son) gets the task. It takes more time to complain about it than to do it, so now, it just gets done.

We use a similar method for laundry. My daughters are at that stage where they do their own laundry now and they have their own system that consists mostly of waiting until they have nothing clean to wear, but for me, I run the washing machine two or three mornings a week. My washing machine judges how much water to use, so I don't have the same hang ups that my mother had about running a full load. I have been known to run a small load just as often as I'll run a load of twelve pairs of jeans that shakes my whole house. I put the clothes in before I leave for work in the morning and when I return home, I'll switch the clothes to the dryer. It seems rather simple, but I tell you, that until I created a system, laundry was the bane of my existence. I could never get a handle on it. It was forever mounting and when I even thought about doing laundry, again, I was disgusted. For a while, I felt like all I did was laundry. And if I wasn't washing clothes, I was fretting the task.

Since then, I've come to terms that I am not a victim to the mass amounts of fabric my family dirties. I find that a lot of my housekeeping struggles came with me into my marriage and over time, I have had to learn to let a lot of things go. I feel like I am more relaxed because of it, whether or not I am or not could be argued by my family. I still have more than my fair share of things that I hold on to, though. For instance, when I'm getting dressed, I like to find my clothes in my closet or my dresser, rather than stuffed into a laundry basket, so I fold the laundry in my bedroom and put my clothes away right then.

I unload the clean laundry right onto my bed – imposing my own rules onto myself. I can't go to bed with a pile of laundry on top of the bed. I suppose I could, but I'd really rather not have to wake up to that mess, so I'm forcing myself to put my clothes away. It takes less than ten minutes, really. I read a statistic that said we spend over seven years of our lives looking for missing items. I figure that putting my laundry away probably saves me three years of my life.

The planner system that I use teaches you how to prioritize your tasks on your To-Do list, but I discovered that there was a flaw in it for me. Whenever I marked an item on my To-Do list with a "C", meaning that the item was low on the priorities of things that had to be done that day, my brain never felt like it was important, so I never got around to it. For me, rather than marking the items with A's, B's and C's, I prefer to keep a running tab. I calendar the items that are important and will take some time to accomplish and I check off the others when I finish them. If it's something that I keep putting off, then I find the best line of defense is to delegate it out to a family member or someone in my office. I often find that the task will get done faster and better than I would've done anyhow– so delegating is a great way to help me prioritize.

I used to have an associate who was uber-organized. I learned so much working with her. She kept a voicemail log and whenever she returned the phone call, she would highlight the message. For her, highlighting the message showed her what she had done without crossing out any information she might need to come back for later. I often found myself on the other phone line when she would call in for a phone number. She had an uncanny memory for recalling the date the message came in. I could easily look up the messages and quickly recite the phone number to her over the phone.

I teach my kids to use checkmarks rather than crossing off items, just in case you need to go back and read through the list. There might be a textbook page or some other detail that could get lost under a crossed-out line, plus, it looks cleaner. There are times when something can't be finished in one sitting. If I start working on an item, but don't finish it, I'll put a dot next to it. That lets me know that it's in progress. I'll mark an X if I decided not to do it or it was canceled and a D if I delegated it out. I find that when I delegate an item out, I still need to follow up to make sure it was completed. I can't feel comfortable checking it off until I know it was actually taken care of. Plus, this keeps me in the loop with whomever I delegated to. They know that I will check in, so they are more apt to stay accountable.

To-Do List

✓	Schedule Eye Appointments
✓	Girl's Haircuts
✓	Marketing Schedule
•	Schedule Meeting with Radio Producer
D	Pull Credit Report
✓	Pay Household Bills
✓	Pay Business Bills

For most people I know, the calendar and the What-To-Do list covers just about everything in keeping an orderly home or office. When it comes time to leaving the office or going on vacation, those are the two items that help me to delegate what needs to be done while I'm gone.

30

I have found that raising a family and owning a business means that I cannot do everything, but I can do something and for those that I can't do, I delegate.

CHAPTER FOUR
The Chore List

I'm a great believer in luck.
I find the harder I work, the luckier I am. – Thomas Jefferson

My daughters were six years old when they were first handed a toilet brush. I was in a rush to get out of the house and I was behind on the chores I wanted to get done. I brought the two of them into the bathroom for a quick demonstration and then sent them off to the other two bathrooms to take care of things. They both did a marvelous job and it opened my eyes to their helpful potential. I had heard of giving children more household responsibility and I myself always had chores to do after school, but until I had a real immediate need, the only help I had expected from them was to clean up their own toys.

When they were two years old, I had dubbed them "the tornadoes" because of the disaster they would leave in any room they were in. When they helped me clean the toilets that day, I felt as if the heavens opened up and shined a light down upon me. Rather than always cleaning up after my little minions, they could be called on to help. Finally!

I started with one chore a day. It included chores like scrubbing toilets, emptying trashcans and dusting. They were young and enthusiastic . . . at first. It required a lot of reminding and they never got to the stage where they just completed their chores without prodding from me. Even though I had to remind them, they always did a pleasant job. I learned to relax on my expectations in favor of the assistance.

Every six months or so, I would add another chore to their list, trying to keep their ability level in mind. We would mix it up – because frankly, keeping on top of the chores could be a chore.

We've tried different incentive methods and even different schedules for doing chores. For a while, Saturday morning was Chore Day. For a few hours, we all worked together to get the big job done, but we finally ended up choosing a daily checklist instead. We would each take fifteen minutes each day after school and work on our chores. Later, it was moved to before school. Since I wanted the chores to take a minimal amount of time, I divided them into simple things that could be done in fifteen minutes or less. We kept this method up for years. Even though my kids are older now and we don't use a chore list anymore, each morning the beds are made, the kitchen is tidied (dishwasher emptied) and the laundry gets done. The chore list actually developed into habits they still use today, but back then, I didn't know that would happen.

Out of necessity, inventions are born and that was how the chore list became a system for my family to keep our house clean. It took a lot of the burden off of me, both with the actual chore, but even with reminding them to clean up after themselves. Because of the chore list, I didn't have to chase after them everyday to put their stuff away and clean up the bathroom, it just got done.

Knowing what my kids were capable of – and how much to expect was the hardest thing for me. I knew what needed to get done, but I wasn't always sure what was age-appropriate. As if my house was bugged for marketers, I found a newspaper clipping with an article from Family Life Magazine called "Chore Wars" and they listed chores that fit each age.

The Chore List (By Age)

Age 3 and 4
Straighten and smooth bed
Pick up toys
Set the table with spoons and forks and plastic ware
Match socks
Help prepare meals (rinse vegetable, stir batter)
Unload silverware from dishwasher (no knives)
Put dirty clothes in laundry basket
Put clean clothes in drawers
Pour dry cereal
Pour pet food into bowls
Wipe table with a sponge
Clean up spills

Ages 5 and 6
Make a standard bed
Straighten room
Set table, complete with glasses and plates
Learn to handle knives
Carry dishes to the sink
Water indoor and outdoor plants
Hand-wash dishes; no knives or glasses
Dust and sweep up crumbs
Prepare snacks, make sandwiches
Pick vegetables in the garden
Feed, walk and brush pets
Help find items at the grocery store
Load and empty the dryer

Ages 7 to 11
Strip a bed and put on fresh sheets
Keep a room clean
Sort and fold laundry
Take out the trash and sort recycling
Rinse dishes and put in dishwasher
Unpack groceries
Mop floors
Vacuum
Learn to do laundry
Shovel snow
Learn to use stove, oven and microwave
Organize coupons
Help prepare grocery list
Scrub bathroom sink, tub and toilet
Pack school lunches
Weed garden
Sew buttons
Learn to use a push mower
Rake leaves
Help watch younger siblings
Polish silverware
Wash the dog

Ages 12 and 13
Babysit
Do laundry
Wash car
Mend clothing
Iron
Change cat litter box
Learn to plan and prepare meals

Ages 14 and up
Learn to use power mower
Learn to use snow blower
Be responsible for preparing one dinner a week
Learn how to prepare several different meals

Later, I clipped out this chart for helping the kids prepare to live on their own:

Skills to know before they leave home
Learn to balance a checkbook and keep a budget
Save money for future expenses
Clean kitchen appliances
Learn to clean out bathroom drains
Change a light bulb
Shop for groceries
Schedule doctor, dentist and other appointments
Manage a schedule

I learned the hard way about how to manage my own schedule right after high school. I had taken an office job at a drain-cleaning company that was five minutes from my house. I felt very mature having an office position because I had always worked either retail or as a receptionist prior to this. I had my own desk and my own phone extension. I felt like a success.

Punctuality had never been a strong suit for me. I had been sent to the principal's office many times for being late to class. I had an English teacher who would lock the door at the bell and either I had to go get a tardy slip or miss the class altogether. Often, I would choose to skip that class, thinking I was proving a point. Oh, the drama of a teenage girl! I brought that poor high school habit with me when I graduated.

My supervisor spoke to me about my tardiness on several occasions and I promised to do better. I only lived five minutes away, how hard could this be? I ended up being fired from that job and I still recall that feeling. It was a tough pill to swallow, but I had to learn it. I was not changing my ways and if I hadn't been fired, I wouldn't be as committed to being on time now. It seems like a lot of the tough lessons are naturally built into life.

At first, I thought of the chore list as a way to get my family to help out around the house. As a stay-at-home mom, it was really easy for me to just do what needed to be done – and often, it seemed easier to do it myself rather than teach my family how to do it. I had a girlfriend who believed in this style. For her, since she chose to be a stay-at-home mom, she took it upon herself to be chief cook and bottle-washer. I knew I didn't want that for myself, but until the chore list came along, that model fit my family, too.

Really, the value in the chore list didn't come until years later, when I discovered that I was teaching my children life-long skills. They were always proud of themselves when they accomplished something and did a job well. They really like it when their room is clean and they can find their toys and books. The accolades were built in, because we all enjoyed the fruits of our labor. We would bake something in the cleaned-up kitchen or sit in the cleaned-up living room and all read books. Nobody likes cleaning up, but we found that we really enjoyed the results.

38

CHAPTER FIVE
The Honey-Do List

No bees, no honey; no work, no money – Traditional Proverb

I find that a Honey-Do List can either be an effective use of delegation, or it can turn into more work. The art of delegation really lies in the follow up. You can't just tell someone else to do something and expect it to get done in your time frame – or even by your standards. You must check in to make sure the assignment was completed and make sure that it didn't leave a wake of new assignments in its path.

At work, there are tasks that are more suited for another person's job description, gifts and talents. I have an assistant who confirms appointments and sends out our correspondence. At home, I have a husband who is more talented at jobs involving landscaping or power tools. I was lucky in the fact that I married a handyman. Jay can fix anything. But Jay isn't the only one I delegate to. I do have the phone number for a plumber, an arborist, a mechanic and a financial planner, to name a few.

Delegating isn't telling someone else to do something you don't want to do. It requires effort on your part. You have to make sure the assignment is clearly understood and you have to make sure everyone agrees to the deadline. You also have to follow up to make sure it was completed.

When I was experimenting with the chore list, I found that I got to be a lot better at discerning what was appropriate and it happened with a lot of trial and error. The Honey-Do List has gone through a lot of similar trials. They say it takes a village to raise a child; I say it takes an entire network of professionals to keep a home while simultaneously running a business. My weekends and days off could easily be sucked up with home improvement projects. And after the last project, I've decided to keep my Honey-Do list to a minimum, whenever I can.

I want to warn you right off the bat. Starting a Honey-Do list can have some backlash. I'm not talking about the resistance you might get from your honey – I'm talking about the aftermath of a project gone bad.

I was sitting on my deck enjoying a cup of coffee and the morning quiet. I began to survey my yard as I noticed the weeds that needed to be pulled and the siding showing its ten-year wear. Jay came outside and we began to make a list of upcoming household projects. The carpet really needs to be replaced and soon, it will be the windows and the kitchen appliances. We'd like to redesign our master bath and the laundry room. The baseboards are all nicked up and the cupboards really need to be re-stained.

We decided to head over to Home Depot and The Great Indoors to spend some pretend-money dreaming about the possibilities. Oh, the great things we could do! We looked at carpeting, tiles, refrigerators and cabinets. We envisioned a new shower and tub with a fabulous vanity. We giggled over the appliances and all the buttons and extra compartments. We compared this one to that one and because we weren't making any decisions, we simply took it all in. It was a leisurely day, full of possibilities.

We ended up at The Container Store, where truly, anything is possible! We made a critical error. We decided to take on a small project; we would install elfa™ drawers for the bathroom cupboards. For ten years, I've wished there were drawers in my bathroom instead of only having cupboards and today, we were making that dream, albeit small, come true.

I like small projects that have a clear end in sight. So often though, household projects seem to take on a life of their own. Once, we thought of replacing the kitchen counter tops. The package included a new sink, so we'd have to replace the faucet, too. And as long as we were buying new counter tops, we should enlarge the island to include the seating we've always wanted. And the backsplash would need to be replaced and what about appliances? Stop! No new counter tops for me!

So this project, drawers for the cupboard, would be small. We should be able to tackle the entire project in one day. It wouldn't grow beyond the boundaries of the cupboard. It was safe. Except that the plumbing was in the way. One more trip to Home Depot to replace the valves with smaller ones. The elfa™ drawers were such a perfect fit, you would think they were custom-designed. They had to be built inside the cupboard and so Jay needed a different hammer. Back to Home Depot.

I cooked dinner as Jay pounded away. He asked for earplugs. I began to clean out the linen closet to keep myself occupied. Funny, an entire closet for linens and it's full of everything but. I emptied it out and filled the entire bathroom with supplies for an army; an army of girls who obviously want curly hair. I found three curling irons, three bags of spongy curlers, two sets of hot rollers, three blow dryers and enough lotion to fill a shopping bag that is now going to the battered women's shelter.

By the time I had finished cleaning out the closet, Jay was also finished. There were beautiful drawers, as if they had been there all along. It was perfect. And it was finished. Oh, wait. Something had happened to the sink. The hammering and rattling had caused the porcelain to chip away from the finish. Now, we need a new sink. Back to Home Depot.

It turns out, that our sink model has been discontinued. Of course it has. So now we have to make some new decisions. Do we buy two new sinks for the master bathroom, so they match each other? Do we pull the sink out of the powder bath, put it into the master bath and replace that one with a new sink? Or do we replace the kid's bathroom sink?

Here's what I'm thinking: If we replace both sinks in the master bath, we then have two brand new matching sinks. It costs twice as much as buying one new sink. If we replace the sink in the powder bath or the kid's bathroom, then we only have to replace one sink, but what if something goes wrong pulling out that sink? Is there a chance that the counter top will be ruined? What about the fixtures? Will we end up replacing a counter top or the faucet? If we replace the counter top, then the paint will have to be redone. It's easier to repaint the kid's bathroom, because its' a single color and the powder bath is a faux-finish that can't be re-matched, even though that counter top would be easier to replace since it's half the size of the kid's bathroom counter. Since the current sink is unusable and we've thought about going down to one sink when we remodel, should we just replace the counter top instead? Of course, if we were going to eliminate that sink in the first place, we wouldn't have needed to replace the valves below to make the elfa™ drawers fit, ruining the sink and we wouldn't be here.

This is all reminiscent of the children's book, *If you give a mouse a cookie*. If you start a household project, then be forewarned, you're going to have to start another one.

Ultimately, we decided to bring up the sink in the powder bath because it matched and Jay thought it offered the path-of-least-new-projects. The powder bath got a new sink, with only one more trip to the hardware store. And they all lived happily ever after.

Currently, here is what is actually on my Honey-Do list.

Paint kitchen baseboard – this winter
Change light bulb in the mudroom – this week
Clean out dryer vent – this month
Stain kitchen bench – this winter
Replace broken knob on stove – this month

I recommend having five or fewer items on a Honey-Do list at one time. If it gets too long, your honey might look at you as if you've gone mad and he won't even know where to begin, at least, that's what I'm told.

It doesn't often occur to my honey to just start at the top and work his way down. He has his own method, usually preferring to start with the tasks that require a shopping trip to Home

Depot and the use of a power tool. All other things tend to get put on the back burner. Did I mention that the knob on the stove needs to be replaced?

CHAPTER SIX
The Money List
(also known as The Budget)

*A budget tells us what we can't afford, but it doesn't keep
us from buying it.* – William Feather

Jay and I started out our married life with two car payments,
several credit cards, a business loan and medical expenses from
the premature birth of our twin daughters. We were a single-
income family, in over our heads financially and we lived in
my parent's basement for our first three and a half years of
marriage. Thank goodness for patient and supportive parents.
My parents invited us to construct an apartment in their
basement to raise our little family in when they knew we didn't
have the financial means to live out on our own. It was a
blessing to have my mom's help when our twin babies were
little. We never dreamed we would live with them for so long,
but when we moved out, we were completely debt-free!

We took it upon ourselves to get out of debt without declaring
bankruptcy and we learned how to save and plan for the future.
For so long, the future meant as long as it took to move into a
house of our own. For years, my budget consisted of a list of
where my money was spent at the end of the month, rather than

a plan for where to spend my money at the beginning of the month. It took awhile for us to "get it". To understand that we are in control of our money never quite sunk in as long as we were using credit cards to get us to the end of the month. Even though we paid off our cards most months out of the year, there was always July (full of family birthdays) and December (full of family parties and gifts) that took us beyond our paycheck.

I had invited a neighbor over for an in-home basket party. When she declined, she told me that she had already created her budget for the month and "baskets" weren't in it. I was curious. How did she know in advance what she would be spending her money on?

Then we took a Dave Ramsey's "Financial Peace" course and became groupies for the concept of saying "no" to using credit cards. Credit card companies really have us confused when it comes to building credit and keeping our FICO score high. The only real benefit to building credit and having a high FICO score is to stay in debt and create more debt.

We build our own snowball of debt to the point where the only way to buy something new is to use debt or credit to do it. It's a snowball that starts out small and manageable, but before you know it, it's rolling out of control. The current economic downfall is mostly affecting those who spend more than they earn. It's so easy to do, plus, we're constantly being encouraged to take part in the over-spending. A well-meaning family member once encouraged us to buy a new car, saying, "it's only a car payment". We couldn't keep up with the bills we had, but off we went to buy a new car. We bought into the credit card and FICO myth hook, line and sinker. And we were caught like a fish on a line.

A well-used budget has kept us from missing mortgage payments, but more importantly, it's kept us from turning an emotional crisis into a simultaneous financial crisis. You know how it goes: there's an unexpected bill and because we didn't plan for it, it's now an emotional crisis *AND* a financial crisis.

It turns out that my neighbor really could anticipate her monthly bills in advance. She wasn't psychic and she didn't own a Magic 8 Ball. It turns out that Christmas *ALWAYS* falls in December and the kids *ALWAYS* return back to school in the fall. Each month, there is always that "something" that comes up. When I looked back at what we spent our money on, I could see a real pattern, an expected pattern of expenses that I could plan for. We have our fixed expenses (mortgage, food, gas) but even the variable expenses weren't all that variable. We all needed haircuts regularly, shoes, school supplies; everything we purchased could be predetermined. Now, maybe I don't always know that we'll be invited out with friends or be given an opportunity to go see the Rockies play at Coors Field– but even those expenses could be anticipated with my MSF: Monthly Something Fund.

The Monthly Something Fund (MSF) started out as a running joke. Each month, we would have to laugh because something would come up that wasn't necessarily planned for. It was so uncanny, yet predictable. There would be an invitation, an event, or a milestone. Each month of the year always has "something". So now, MSF is a budgeting category for us.

There are a lot of budgeting tools on the Internet and most of my favorites are found at DaveRamsey.com. He recommends a zero-based balance – and simply put, that means that you give every dollar a name at the beginning of the month. If you don't have a name for it – then you don't spend it. It takes some discipline to realize that a budget isn't a Nazi-force keeping you from having a good time, but an ally to help you achieve your financial goals. Benjamin Franklin said that a penny saved is a penny earned.

I didn't want my family to live paycheck to paycheck back when we were receiving them every two weeks. I wanted more security than that. I wanted to know that if the paychecks stopped, we could still make our mortgage payment – without using a home equity loan. I didn't want to have to call the bank everyday to check on my available balance. I didn't want creditors to ever call on me again like they did after my daughters were born. I didn't want to be in a position of thinking that my answer was in the next loan that someone may or may not approve. I want to be self-insured rather than paying for silly warranties that cost my family money. I want to be able to pay one check at the beginning of the year for my trash service and earn a discount. I want to be in a position to negotiate for better rates because I pay cash. I found that when I was behind the eight-ball in debt, I could never get ahead. Late fees, interest charges, overdraft fees and monthly payment fees all add up to money that was keeping me from my own dreams and goals.

To get a quick head start, we picked one month to set the foundation. Jay and I went on a spending fast. We stopped all non-essential spending for one month. We made interesting meals out of the supply we had in the full pantry and freezer. We didn't go out to eat; we only drove the car to work to save on gas and we told the kids to find creative ways to stay entertained. We went for walks to the park and to the library. As a mother, the library has always been one of my favorite places to take the kids. It's the one place I get to say "yes" to them. The library has movies, books, music and games. When they ask me, "Mommy, can I get this book?" My answer is "yes". When they ask, "can we get both movies?" My answer is "yes". When I would take them to the mall or to the grocery store, I felt like I was constantly saying "no", but at the library, I get to say "yes" over and over again. The library is truly one of my favorite places to take my children. There's no doubt that this has had a significant impact on them. They are all insatiable readers and creative writers.

For the month, we went through our own closets and re-gifted. We had a garage sale and earned some extra cash. We sold a few things on eBay and we made a pact to get through one month of no-spending. It was a challenge that we all took together. I really appreciated my kids getting on board with us and I told them so. We had to turn down requests from friends. We had to get really creative after the second week of no grocery shopping; potatoes with canned corn and peanut butter on crackers. But we didn't starve and we didn't die.

We took our savings and our extra earnings and created an emergency fund. We began to pay our mortgage one month in advance, as well as our other expenses. And we took control. There's nothing like that feeling. It's absolutely exhilarating.

For the last two years, we've signed up for the refresher course that Financial Peace offers. It keeps Jay and me on the same page – as well as the kids because we come home from the class all excited about what we learned and we share it with them. We find that it's really, really easy to get distracted and we tend to want to spend more than we earn. We know that this is one of our weak areas so we do what we can to stay on top of it.

The Dave Ramsey site has all the budget worksheets you need to get started, but the ones we use are the ones I created myself using an Excel spreadsheet. For three months, I kept track of every penny that we spent and created a budget for the next month. I started with budgeting for one month at a time. I planned in advance for every category. When I first started, I had twenty different categories. Today, I have fifteen. A budget has to be fluid. It has to work with my family and not against it. Fortunately, Jay and I have the same *frugability* quotient. We like to spend on the same things and we like to save for the same things. We made up the word 'frugability' after listening to some friends complain to each other how they were spending their money. It turns out, Jay and I are equally yoked in the frugability department. Taking the Financial Peace course together as a couple has really helped with that.

<Frugability \frü•ga•bil•etë\ *adv* : sharing the same thrifty desires>

It helps to have an outsider teaching you to have an emergency fund in place. It's neither my idea nor Jay's idea, so we don't have to argue over it. We do it because Dave Ramsey says to. When Jay quit his job, we didn't reduce the amount we were contributing to our IRA, even though it seemed like we should be saving every penny just in case we needed it to pay the mortgage. Since we had been disciplined into saving and planning for retirement, the system was already in place, so we continued our savings plan. To this day, we haven't had to compromise on that.

Here is a sample list of budgeting categories along with some recommended percentages, as found on the Dave Ramsey website. Remember, there may be extra categories here that you don't need and the percentages are recommendations only. If you have an unusually high or unusually low income, these percentages are way off. They are based on an annual salary of $40,000. If you earn three times that much, you probably don't want to spend $1500.00 a month on groceries.

Budgeting Categories

10-15%	Charitable Giving
5-10%	Taxes
25-35%	Housing (first and second mortgage, HOA fees, taxes and insurance)
5-10%	Utilities (electricity, water, gas, phone, trash, cable)
5-15%	Food (groceries and eating out)
10-15%	Transportation (payment, fuel, maintenance, insurance, license and taxes)
5-10%	Insurance (disability, health, life)
3-10%	Education (childcare, tuition, school supplies)
3-10%	Entertainment (movies, going out, travel)
3-10%	Recreation (gym memberships, hobby equipment, park passes)
3-10%	Clothing (including dry cleaning and tailoring)
3-10%	Savings (emergency fund, retirement fund, college fund)
3-10%	Medical (co-payments, medication, doctor/dental bills)
3-10%	Home Improvement (repairs and maintenance)
3-10%	Personal Care (toiletries, salon visits, cosmetics)
3-10%	Gifts (birthdays, teachers, Christmas)
3-10%	Credit Cards & Loans (include. Child support and alimony)
3-10%	MSF (monthly something fund)

To help you get a head start on your budget, here is a list of money savers that also happen to have a secondary benefit, either by helping you create a healthier lifestyle or by strengthening your relationships with those you love.

26 Ways to Save Money

1. Install a Smart Power Strip that will turn off the passive electricity going to all of your electronic devices, saving you money on your electric bill. Plug this into a surge protector to keep from having to replace damaged electronics. Ka-ching, more money stays in your wallet.

2. Utilize online bill paying to spend less on stamps, boxed checks and late fees.

3. Add a 30-minute daily walk to your schedule to eliminate health club fees and keep your heart strong. Most people underestimate the value of walking. This is like investing in your future. Your activity today will save you in the long run.

4. Rent movies for $1.00 a day and cut out your cable and satellite channels.

5. Ask for fees to be waived. They won't offer, but will often comply to reduce fees, if they can. Ask for reduced interest charges, rate reductions and discounts.

6. Use your library resources. Books, movies, music and games are all available at your local library. You can use the Internet, learn a foreign language, attend free concerts and stay aware of what's going on in your

community. You can get rid of your magazine subscriptions and check out magazines at your local library.

7. Slow down. Traffic violations are a stupid and avoidable drain on your budget.

8. Find one hundred uses for vinegar to reduce your expenses on household cleaning items.

9. Buy cars that are three to five years old. They are practically brand new at a fraction of the cost.

10. Repair instead of replace. This works on household and clothing items. Ask for help from a friend or a neighbor and you also create a great bonding experience while saving your budget.

11. Use your Crock Pot. Dinner is ready when everyone is hungry and you can cut down your restaurant bills.

12. Carpooling reduces maintenance costs, fuel usage, and is better for your relationships all while doing something good for the environment.

13. Consider your public transportation system for commuting to work. You'll cut back on parking costs and even use that time to catch up on items you can't do while driving.

14. Brown-bag for lunch. You can eat healthier and save a ton of cash by packing your lunch the night before. Remember to take it with you!

15. Swap babysitting with friends. Give the gift of your talents instead of gifts that will end up in someone's garage sale. Pet sitting, lawn care, home-cooked meals all say, "I care about you" much more than any item you could purchase at the mall.

16. Give consumable gifts to teachers instead of collectibles and things that will add clutter to their lives. You can make your own cookies, breads, soaps, candles, and layered brownie mixes. Add a personal note and it will mean more than anything you could purchase and it will save your wallet, too.

17. Quit the shopping-hobby. If you don't see it, you won't miss all of those great bargains.

18. Use a shopping list to reduce impulse shopping and save yourself money at the checkout stand.

19. Eliminate your "collections". Collections are a representation of the money you spent on something that now collects dust instead of interest.

20. Invite friends over instead of going out. Potluck and a deck of cards will keep everyone entertained much cheaper than a bar tab.

21. Volunteer your time. You'll save yourself money while you're busy giving to others.

22. Switch to term life insurance. For a fraction of the cost, you can have better life insurance coverage. Insurance is not an investment tool.

23. Wash your hands. Keep your family germ-free and you'll reduce doctor bills, medicines and time off from work.

24. Drink more water. Great health and financial benefits every time you sip.

25. Go vintage. Purchasing used sports equipment, video games, books and movies will save you a significant amount of cash. Consignment stores, garage sales, even your neighbor's basement are full of treasures you would be willing to pay full price for at the mall.

26. Turn off the television. You'll view less guilt-inducing advertisements that cost you money later. You'll reduce the mindless "t.v. watching" snacking and keep your waist trimmer. You'll discover you have more free time to volunteer, catch up on projects or spend time with those you love playing games or going for a walk.

CHAPTER SEVEN
The Ultimate Packing List

When preparing to travel, lay out all your clothes and all your money. Take half the clothes and twice the money.
— Susan Heller

When we decided to plan a trip to Europe, the whole thing took on a life of its own. For the prior ten years, I had worked for a PGA golf tournament and worked full time every summer. The kids were on year-round schedules and they only got three weeks off during the summer. We hadn't been on a summer vacation in ten years. Jay's schedule was so flexible; he could be around before and after school, while the tournament prepared to come to town. I loved my position with the tournament and it worked out really well to have the kids rely on dad for a few weeks instead of me.

After twenty-one years on the tour, the tournament had been cancelled. That same year, Jay's company was making significant changes and was getting ready to close. He had accumulated over five weeks of vacation that he needed to use and Alycia and Lauren were on a traditional school schedule now that they were in middle school. Michael would have to miss a few weeks of school, but since he was an excellent student, we thought he could handle the departure. The stars had aligned and we were heading to Europe!

We knew that we wanted to rely on public transportation so it was important that everyone be able to handle his/her own luggage. We couldn't rely on daddy to carry all the bags on and off the trains and airplanes for everyone. From a previous vacation, we also knew that our large suitcases didn't fit in the subway turnstiles. They say that he who travels happily must travel light.

We decided that each of us would be in charge of our own suitcase, so we purchased large rolling duffle bags. They didn't weigh much, they would fit in the turnstiles and each one of us could wheel our own piece of luggage around. The next challenge was, "what do you pack?"

We were going to be gone for five total weeks, traveling in Italy, Spain, France and the United Kingdom. I had read a story about a couple who had backpacked through Europe with only one extra change of clothes in their backpack. Each day, they would walk from town to town and when they arrived at their hotel each night, they would wash their outfit from the day and hang it up to dry.

They would wear their clean outfit out to dinner and for the next day's travel. It fascinated me to think someone could travel so lightly. It caused quite a stir when I pitched the idea to my family. It was more extreme than we wanted to go, but we found a way to compromise. We agreed to each take only five outfits. Now, this packing list has become the foundation for all of our trips and with a few modifications, it even works for camping trips.

Keep in mind; we knew that we would be renting homes, each with a washing machine. We didn't realize that our dryer was going to be a clothesline – but in its novelty, we managed to hang our socks and underwear discreetly between t-shirts and towels.

The Ultimate Packing List covers the clothing needs for just about any standard family vacation. We modify as necessary.

One outfit to lounge and sleep in.

This outfit consists of lounge pants and a t-shirt. We could put this on after the pool, after a long travel day and then sleep in it. Rather than slippers for the tile floors, we wore our Crocs™ with socks.

One outfit to wear to the beach or pool.

As a matter of rule, whenever we go on a trip, we always pack a swimsuit, whether we think we'll need it or not. It doesn't take up any room at all, yet, in a pinch, it's almost impossible to replace. You can't always borrow one or find one at the store in an off season – so we consider a swimsuit to be a packing-staple. For this trip, we knew that each home we were renting had its own swimming pool. The pool outfit consists of a swimsuit and a t-shirt for the boys and a sundress/cover up for the girls. When we went to Hawaii, we discovered that this was our daily outfit and we hardly wore anything else. For footwear, we wore our Crocs™ to the beach and to the pool.

Two outfits for sightseeing.

Whenever you're traveling, you want to have something nice to wear out to a restaurant, museum or other activities where you will be seen in public. In Europe, we wanted to blend in, so we didn't pack jeans. Besides, they are also heavy to carry. Even though jeans hide the dirt and it seems like they would be the perfect traveling pant, they are difficult to wash in small washing machines and they take forever to dry. We chose to pack two pair of pants (khaki and navy blue) for the boys and skirts and a pair of Capri pants for the girls. Each outfit included their own shirts that all coordinated with each other. On any given day, you could mix and match. We knew that we would be going to see Il Divo in concert while we were in Paris, so one of the outfits was appropriate for that. I threw in a pashmina scarf to dress up my outfit for that night. The boys had a pair of walking shoes (loafer-style) and the girls all had a sandal-type shoe.

One travel day outfit.

In between each country, we would be spending almost twenty four hours traveling. Our travel day outfit included a rain jacket and an ensemble that was comfortable to travel in. Non-wrinkle pants and a long-sleeved solid colored t-shirt kept us warm inside air-conditioned airplanes, buses and trains. We all wore our Crocs™ on this day. For comfort and ease of taking shoes off and on at security checks, they were great. We picked dark, neutral colors and to this day, they are my favorite shoe to travel in.

We each had our own suitcase and a travel bag that kept a book, snacks and other comfort items. I kept the itinerary and we all had a puzzle book (Sudoku, crosswords) and the kids brought their handheld electronic games. Of course, our battery charger blew its fuse in Italy so the kids went ten full days without their electronic games until we found a new charger in Spain.

Each suitcase weighed less than fifteen pounds, except for Jay's. He carried a few more items and his bag weighed less than twenty five pounds.

The Ultimate Packing list can be altered to fit your schedule. For example, when we went camping, we packed one lounger, one swimwear and two outfits that included jeans, a t-shirt and a sweatshirt. The Ultimate Packing list makes it easy for my kids to pack on their own. They add underwear and socks for each outfit and include any accessories they like and we're quickly packed and on our way.

There were parts of our trip where we felt like we had packed too many clothes. For example, when we were in Spain, we lived in the swimming pool or at the beach and only wore our sightseeing outfit once in the seven days we were there. When we were in Paris, I found that I was doing a load of laundry every day, but it was a small load and manageable, so it wasn't a big deal.

We had to be really careful about buying souvenirs because we were going to be hauling them all over Europe, so our packing system even helped us from buying silly things we wouldn't want later. In Italy, the girls each bought long flowy linen skirts and in Paris, they each bought a hoody-sweatshirt. Both items got a lot of wear after the trip, so they were great investments. Michael bought a new t-shirt in Paris and overall, our souvenir expenses were minimal. I did get very excited in the hardware store in Paris, though. I love the shops and boutiques in other countries, but Paris is my favorite. I love how everyone greets each other as you enter and exit. It makes you want to spend your money in their establishment. But I was careful. I already had a full bag.

The Ultimate Packing List

✓	1	Lounge/Sleeping Outfit
✓	1	Pool/Beach Outfit
✓	1	Travel Day Outfit
✓	2	Sightseeing Outfit (mix and match)

CHAPTER EIGHT
The Shopping List

*It is more fun to talk with someone who doesn't use long,
difficult words but rather short, easy words like
"How about lunch?"* - Winnie the Pooh

As a typical stay-at-home with young children, going grocery shopping meant bringing the kiddos along to the grocery store while daddy was at work. I would pack the kids into the cart and creatively manage to pack the groceries in all around them. We would traverse the aisles and every other minute, one of the three was asking for something. "Ooh, can we have that? How about this? We haven't had those in a long time," or, "I really want these!"

One time, I calculated that is cost me an extra $40.00 to take the kids along to the grocery store, so I started going alone. I did all the shopping alone until my husband started questioning my spending behaviors. He would question the amount as well as some of my choices. We got into a pretty hilarious spat over my purchase of $3.00 on disposable cups for the bathroom. I was grossed out by the toothpaste caked on the cup the kids had been using in the bathroom and with the sudden outburst of the cold virus, I thought the $3.00 purchase was wise. My husband, however, felt like my shopping hobby was nickel and diming our family into debt. He felt like my frequent trips to Wal-Mart and Target were destroying our budget. He argued that my small purchases were adding up to too much money being spent on items our family really didn't need. Small leaks sink ships, he told me.

We were both right. The toothpaste-crusted cup was gross and the disposable cups would keep germs from spreading, but the cups were actually a symbol of a bigger problem at our house. My shopping hobby meant that I was buying things because they were a good deal more often than because it was an item our family actually needed. I could walk into a discount store and buy twenty different items, each under $5.00 and still spend $100.00. Even though I wasn't purchasing big ticket items, I was still spending a lot of money every month. And when I would try to itemize our budget, I had to add a column called Wal-Mart/Target. I had a column for clothing, food and household items, but at these stores, it could be anything from socks to toilet paper to photo development. A receipt with twenty different items could be divided into twenty different categories, so to save time and energy, I just lumped it all into one category. Our biggest expense every month was in that category and it was out of control.

To make sure that Jay and I were on the same page and also to prove to him that it really is that expensive to make purchases for a family of five, we decided to start doing the shopping together.

All week long, I keep a magnetic shopping list on the refrigerator. Everybody is encouraged to write on the list and even though its primary goal is for groceries, we also include things like socks, shampoo, notebook paper, batteries, a pair of black pants for band or a new belt for Michael. If it needs to be purchased, we write it on the list. At first, the kids would wait until we ran out of cereal or popcorn before they would write something on the list – but they have learned that when the shampoo is running low, it's best to put it on the list, because I only shop once a week now. If you run out, it's because it wasn't on the shopping list. I ask them to be very specific. Once, they put ice cream on the list and I stood freezing in the ice cream aisle trying to make a decision on a flavor everyone would like. I bought vanilla. While this is my personal favorite, I found out that they wanted me to buy the same flavor I had bought before, but no one could remember what it was called because we threw the container away and it had been on special. The same goes for cereal. Be careful when you write 'cereal' on the list because mom will buy something *she* wants or become too overwhelmed with choices and not buy any cereal at all.

When Jay and I go grocery shopping, we purchase from the list rather than purveying the sale signs. It's very different than how I used to go shopping. Before, I would look for the sale items and then stock up. My cupboards were always full of extras. I didn't only have one can of shaving crème in the shower; there were always two or three more in the cupboard. Last week, my friend bought six bottles of Windex because it was on sale and she had a coupon. That used to be me. Now, I've learned that I don't need to tie up my money to save three dollars.

I have one of the large warehouse stores near my home and once a month or so, I would shop there for the deals you get by buying in bulk. I would buy my paper products by the truckload and jarred pasta sauce by the case. In our house prior to this one, I had an area in the basement with shelving and a large standup freezer. Whenever I needed something, I found it stocked in my own basement grocery aisle.

On our first vacation to Europe, we rented a small apartment with a refrigerator the size of a dorm-room fridge. It didn't hold very much and we shopped in the market every day on the way back to the apartment. A couple weeks after we came home, I was standing in front of my freezer full of food and did a rough calculation of how much money was invested in my pantry and freezer. I figured that there was over $500.00 just sitting in my house, just in case. Keep in mind, I live in the suburbs. There are two grocery stores less than two miles from my house. I made a command decision; instead of planning for every 'what if' scenario, I decided to try shopping for only what I really needed to consume that week. I didn't want to change my lifestyle to go shopping every single day, but I figured that I could fit it in once a week. I gave it a trial run.

I created a menu for the week, attempting to use up our existing inventory and I only bought the few items that I needed to supplement the meals. I used my shopping list and I didn't look for sale items to stock up on.

Creating the menu caused a bonus benefit that I wasn't expecting. Having the menu on the fridge for everyone to see created a sense of comfort. No one asks anymore "mom, what's for dinner?" Instead, they look at the menu on the fridge and on most nights, they will even attempt to help me by pulling out the items to de-frost or by starting the pot of rice. It's been fabulous. Menu planning and keeping a shopping list has saved time, money and nagging. Who knew?

Each Sunday we plan our menu and create a shopping list and then Jay and I head to the grocery store. We stop to buy a latte at the coffee bar inside the grocery store and we make a date out of it. The baristas who work there recognize us and have memorized our order. We get to feel like we live in a small town where everybody knows our name. Most couples go out to dinner for their dates but once a week, Jay and I go out for coffee and groceries. We find great value in this time. We are doing something for our family as well as for our relationship. It gives us time to talk to each other and catch up. We get to talk without the kids eavesdropping and we have found that in the long run, we now spend less money on groceries.

I used to think that I needed to clip coupons, buy in bulk and search the sales in order to reduce our grocery bill. What I found is, after two years of buying only what we need versus what's on sale, we spend about twenty five percent less on our grocery bill. I can look back to October 2007 and see that we spent $646.00 on groceries and in October 2008 and 2009, we spent just over $400.00. Even though we might spend more on an item because it's not on sale, I'm only buying what we need to eat that week, so I'm not spending money to store food anymore. We have evolved past being squirrels who stock up for the winter and we put our savings in our retirement accounts instead.

When I'm planning my menu and grocery list, I first try to use up the items that I already have on stock that didn't get consumed the week before. Next, I try to include as many of these powerful ingredients into my menu:

Extra Virgin Olive Oil
Tomatoes
Spinach
Broccoli
Bell Peppers

68
Blueberries
Strawberries
Red Grapes
Almonds
Whole Grains
Skinless Poultry

According to the book, *The Sonoma Diet* these are the top foods they recommend incorporating more into your diets because they deliver the maximum disease-fighting nutrients with a minimum amount of calories. They are the foods that are famous for limiting heart disease and keeping a trim waistline. I try to incorporate as many of these items into my menu as possible. Most can go straight from the farm to the table, so to speak, and that seems like a very healthy choice to me. Plus, they are colorful and pretty.

I once told an audience of women that when it comes to diet and exercise, focus on the 'pretty' factor. It was a very girlie comment, as I tend to be. The word 'pretty' can be taken wrong – as if women who are pretty aren't smart. When you look deep inside the hearts of most women with whom I am friends, you'll find that we all want to feel pretty. Whether or not someone else validates it is not as important as how we feel about ourselves, but it's nice to receive a compliment once in a while.

In this group, we were talking about diet and exercise and I suggested that we should eat foods that are *pretty* (see the list) and do activities that are *pretty*. Dancing, biking, yoga, swimming and jogging are all very pretty exercises if you enjoy doing them. If you frown and are extremely uncomfortable doing an exercise, then you should exchange it for something that makes you smile and that you look forward to doing. If you are currently involved with an exercise program that bores you or is not interesting to you, then it's not pretty and there's probably something you would rather be doing. One gal was complaining that she hated doing lunges. Well, complaining is not very pretty, so we suggested that she stop doing lunges and go for a hike or a bike ride instead. She thought it was brilliant because it was so simple.

My mom finds my grocery shopping method quite unconventional, as do most people who hear about it, but only my mom has real access to my pantry. You can't open my pantry and make every single dish you've ever learned how to cook. You will only find the ingredients for that week's menu. It takes the burden off of making that dinner decision every day. There are days that I forget to start the slow cooker and we end up making grilled cheese sandwiches. There are days when we go out to eat or we switch entrees, but after awhile, you figure out the kinks and still end up with leftover items in the pantry. Right now, there are a couple extra boxes of spaghetti, a package of macaroni and cheese and two cans of tuna. In the freezer, there are a couple packages of frozen ground turkey, ice cream and a bag of frozen chicken breasts. The amazing thing is that the cupboard is never bare. Never. We keep trying to empty it – and we did finally empty the large freezer, but I've never been able to completely clear out the pantry and fridge. It's quite amazing.

I've had friends tell me that this would never work in their house because they don't know what they're going to feel like eating on any given night. I don't either. I choose dishes that I know I like to eat and maybe one night I'm more in the mood for tacos rather than spaghetti, but it's rarely been an issue for us. It's more of a relief to *not* to have to decide what to eat when every one is already hungry.

We reduced our grocery spending to four hundred and fifty dollars a month for a family of five. I don't have a Wal-Mart/Target column in my budget anymore. In fact, I rarely shop at those two stores anymore and I definitely don't go in unless I have a list. My daughters use a special contact lens cleaner that I buy at Wal-Mart and I have been known to go in and buy that one item and leave. In my past life, when I shopped as a hobby, that never happened. I would go in for an item or two and walk out with a shopping cart full of items.

Of course, before school started, I took my school supply list and took the kids shopping at Wal-Mart because where else could I one-stop shop for school supplies, a pair of black pants for Michael to wear for band concerts, a belt and jewelry cleaner? I only wanted to make one stop since I had the kids with me and I went to where I knew I could get everything on my list.

I've discovered that if I shop around to burn time or just to see what they have, I will find something to buy that I didn't even know I was wanting in the first place. When I do that, I take money out of our budget that could be spent on more necessary things like braces and car repairs or paying extra on my mortgage. By using the shopping list, I've helped my family plan ahead for items we know we're running low on and I spend less overall. This is good for my family.

I've quit the shopping hobby and I've taught my family how to shop smarter, too. The menu and the shopping list have made such a positive impact, that I now give magnetic shopping lists as gifts.

CHAPTER NINE
Birthday Card List

Take care of all your memories,
for you cannot re-live them. – Bob Dylan

My sister, Jenn is great at remembering to send out birthday cards or cards for special occasions. She has a special knack for choosing the most perfect card to send to someone and I'm sure she spends countless hours in the card store because her cards are always so perfect for the recipient. I have been blessed on many occasions from the cards she has sent to me. I'm amazed at how personal her cards are. I, on the other hand, tend to leave it to my system.

My system started with a list of birthdays and anniversaries stapled to a manila folder. I would store birthday cards that I bought in a multi-pack inside the folder and on the first of the month, I would mail out birthday and anniversary cards. I found that even a blank or generic card could be spiced up with a personal sentiment. If I can, I try to include a personal memory in the card. I try to be specific with compliments. The more specific you can be, the more meaningful the card is. More important than what I wrote, my friends were grateful that I remembered. But here's the thing, I didn't actually remember. I could usually recall the month, but I surely don't remember all the specific dates, but my birthday list has a great memory. My birthday list makes me look like a hero.

I receive the most comments by sending birthday cards to clients. As we get older, we celebrate this milestone less and less. Every year, I receive fewer and fewer birthday cards from friends and family, but there are a few companies that still value the sentiment of sending out birthday cards to their clients. I love that my company is one of them.

I think that anytime you can send a personalized note to someone is special. It doesn't matter what the occasion is, really, but the sentiment that comes from thinking about someone else for a change is so gratifying. You think that you're sending the card to them because you want them to feel special, but the reality is, when you stop your world from spinning for a moment and you pause to remember something special to say to someone else, the warmth resonates from deep inside and you end up being the one who benefits.

It reminds me of an episode of the sitcom, *Friends*, where Phoebe is searching for any selfless act that didn't also reward the giver. Instead, she finds something selfish in all of them. She allowed herself to be stung by a bee, but discovered that it was selfish because the bee probably died. While it's true; when you do something for someone else, there is an internal benefit but it's a backwards way of looking at it. When you proceed with purely selfish motivation, no one benefits. When you are selfless, everyone benefits.

Sending out birthday cards is a lost art in correspondence, especially with e-cards and Facebook e-gifts and all the other quick and easy electronic methods. However, when you take the time to hand-address an envelope, put a real stamp on it and slip it in the mailbox, you are guaranteeing to make someone's day. A handwritten envelope is guaranteed to get open while, more than half of all e-cards sent are never viewed. A birthday card will take center stage on a desk or on a countertop. They are coveted. Send cards often. What takes you only a few minutes can really make a lasting impact.

As I run low, I'll add birthday cards to my shopping list. I'll go out and purchase a pack of birthday cards or blank cards from the card store and then I'll keep them in a small file box in my desk. At the beginning of the month, I take a few minutes to fill them out. This isn't a time-consuming task. If nothing else, it's a great way to escape from the whirl of the world. Brew a cup of coffee or tea, grab your favorite writing pen and ponder what to say to the person. I have created a list of over fifty opening phrases (see below) that I refer to whenever I get stuck on how to start. I find it's helpful to open with an enthusiastic statement. And I try not to repeat myself; otherwise, it looks like I'm just trying to fill empty space. I sign the card, seal it and then I take a walk to the mailbox. You'll be surprised at how good this all feels. It's like wrapping the world in love notes.

If the birthday doesn't fall until later in the month, sometimes I'll put a sticky note on the card and hold onto it for a couple weeks before mailing it. Most of the time, I'll go ahead and mail cards early. I figure that early is better than later. My kids have a bumper sticker on their bulletin board that reads, "Better late than never, but never late is better." Having a birthday list keeps me off the "never late" list.

My company sends out handwritten thank you cards to all of our clients. With the electronic age of instant messaging, emails and newsletters, a card in the mail really stands out. This year, my company only received one Halloween card, so there was no competition for that business. They were the only one who took the time to send me a handwritten card.

It's really easy to sit at your computer and jot out a quick "thank you" email, but it doesn't really stand out. I ask audiences all the time, "How many emails do you receive on a daily basis?" The answers vary anywhere from twenty five to two hundred and fifty emails in a given day. That's a lot of emails. But, when I counter that question with "How many handwritten cards do you receive every single day?" their faces get all scrunched up as they try to recall the last time that happened. Your quick 'thank you' email may or may not be opened and read, depending on how busy the recipient is. When you send a handwritten card to your clients, you can guarantee that the card will be opened, read and more often than not, shown around. Most cards go on display on top of desks and countertops and then afterwards, they are saved. You can't say that about an email. A handwritten card is treasured.

I'm emphasizing that cards should be handwritten. Your own handwriting is unique to you. It's a special touch that most people underestimate these days. I hear excuses for it all the time: I don't have time or my handwriting is messy.

My orthodontist office opened my eyes to how easy it is to write out a quick note to someone. In their waiting area, they have a small writing desk along with couches and chairs. At the writing desk, they keep a display rack with various blank note cards for anyone to use. While I was waiting for my kids to have their braces adjusted, I would look through my calendar and see who I had visited with recently and I would write out a quick note to them thanking them for their time or the visit and telling them that I appreciate them. I could write out three or four cards without taking any time at all. I started to implement that concept into something more intentional. I could send out three or four cards every day and that would equal up to sixty or eighty cards a month. In my business, keeping my brand in front of sixty or eighty customers a month creates very loyal customers.

I used to work for a company where the executives each had an assistant. The assistant would write out the cards and the executives would sign them. It could be the same way in your company. You could hire someone to write your cards for you. What if you took away the excuses and tried it for awhile? What kind of impact would you have on your relationships? I like receiving cards in the mail. It sure beats the invoices and advertisements that I get now. Hallmark says, "when you care enough to send the very best". I think that sending handwritten cards tells the recipient that you care.

Here's my list of opening statements. These aren't only for birthday wishes, but for any note card to say, I was thinking about you:

I was thinking about you.
You're special.
I'm so glad I know you.
I'm grateful for you.
You're important to me.
I'm so lucky to know you.
Happy birthday.
You're a real trooper.
Your contribution is important.
Great job.
Way to go.
Nice work.
I couldn't have done it without you.
I applaud you.
You encourage others.
You are trustworthy.
You create possibilities.
You're on top of things.
Job well done.
I'm truly grateful.
You inspire me.
You're a winner.
You are a joy to work with.
It is a pleasure working with you.
Hip Hip Hooray!
I'm impressed.
No one holds a candle to you.
Bravo!
Great work!
You are spectacular.

You are incredible.
You are thorough.
Your work is always complete.
Your actions are so thoughtful.
You are innovative.
You are so creative.
You are professional.
Your ideas are powerful.
You are imaginative.
Kudos.
Well done.
I admire you.
You are terrific.
Hurray for you.
You make our company look good.
You are a team player.
I'm proud of you.
You make people feel welcome.
You are fun to work with.
I'm glad I know you.
You are a great example for others.
You are super.
You are unstoppable.
I appreciate you.
I appreciate your work.
I enjoy working with you.
You are a treasure.
You made my day.
You are a caring person.
You are supportive.
I value you.
You make people feel important.
Thank you.

78

CHAPTER TEN
The Dream List

*The future belongs to those who believe in the
beauty of their dreams.* –Eleanor Roosevelt

The dream list is a list of goals that I set for myself. It's kind
of like having a "Bucket List". There is a Hollywood movie out
about a man who set up a list of things he wanted to
accomplish before he kicked the bucket. It was a list of dreams.
Setting goals is like giving myself the gift of dreaming. After I
read the book *The Dream Manager*, I was even more motivated
to talk about goal setting. It's so easy to stop dreaming and
give up on goals. I'm often scoffed at because of my visionary
thinking. I know that sometimes my dreams are way bigger
than I am, but so what? People are really quick to point out to
me why my dreams can't come true – especially if they are
afraid that my big dreams will take me away from them. There
are those who have given up on dreaming and they don't want
to see others achieve success. It can be a very sad state of
affairs.

The Dream Manager prompted me to focus more on personal
goals, especially with my corporate clients. Having goals and

dreams that inspire and challenge ourselves is what separates us from the animal kingdom. We are meant to dream. Goals and dreams help us tolerate that dead-end job while putting ourselves through school. They help us sacrifice today so we can live a better life tomorrow. Putting your dreams and goals down on paper is just like breathing life into them. I'm sure you've heard this before; people who write down their dreams are more likely to achieve them. It's a fact.

On the first of January, I pull out my brand new calendar and Jay and I sit down together with a cup of coffee and review our annual goals. We've been setting goals together almost all of our married years and before we set new goals, we look back to see what we've achieved. It's really funny to look back at goals we set ten years ago and see what was important to us then and compare it to now. There are some things that never change and some things that always change. We can look back and see when we made a commitment to eat dinner together as a family every night (at our pediatrician's recommendation) and what we wanted to do with annual bonuses (usually a family vacation). Setting goals brings back that childhood spirit buried inside of you when you still believed that anything was possible.

Goals are the ultimate motivator for bringing excitement and energy into life. Whenever I feel like I don't have any direction or that I'm just going through the motions, I can almost always pinpoint it back to the fact that I wasn't moving towards a goal. On the contrary, there have been some goals that we've set that have seemed so far out of reach, but our intense motivation and passion for the goal brought it to reality.

We've set some outlandish goals for ourselves from time to time. Taking our family on a five-week trip to Europe was one of those far-reaching goals that required the five of us to stick together to make our dream come true. Another big goal was when we decided to pay for the girl's orthodontia treatment in advance, in cash. Again, it took dedication and sacrifice. When we walked into the dentist's office carrying a briefcase full of nine thousand dollars in one-dollar bills, we checked off another dream. I never realized how much nine thousand one dollar bills would weigh. We didn't weigh it (I don't own a scale) but let me tell you, that briefcase was heavy.

We had made a concrete decision to not go into debt. One of Dave Ramsey's tips says that being able to afford something is not the same as being able to afford the payments. If you can't afford to buy it, to pay for it without missing other bills, you can't afford it. Period. We decided that if we were going to pay for braces, we were going to pay for it in full– and not use credit to do it. Alycia and Lauren had to wait an extra year while we saved up, but it was covered. The orthodontist was expecting me to write a check or put the tab on our credit card. Writing a check for nine thousand dollars doesn't have the same emotional impact as counting it out, one-dollar bill at a time. Nine thousand dollars is a lot of money and it was a serious commitment for my family. I think that we can be so cavalier when it comes to big ticket spending and it's scary how much more socially acceptable it is to be in debt rather than pay for items in full and with cash. With nine thousand actual dollars sitting in front of us, our whole family was committing to this priority.

Setting financial priorities is a valuable lesson that we want our children to glean from us. We spent our early-married years in debt and living in my parent's basement because of it. Our kids still might have to learn this lesson the hard way, but at least we've given them a solid foundation. Jay and I didn't have that. We didn't have anyone to guide us in making solid financial decisions. Neither of our parents had that legacy passed on to them, they didn't need to. Americans have never been as gripped by as much consumer debt as they are today. By choosing to live debt free, Jay and I are starting a new legacy for our family that we didn't start out with.

Most goals have a financial component attached to them, so getting a grip on this area of our lives has had a significant impact on making our dreams come true. Not every goal is financial, though. We have broken it down into five categories; spiritual, home improvement, family, personal and financial.

Spiritual Goals

Jay and I tell people that we met in the Amway business. That's true. In our Amway group, there was a couple that invited us to attend a brand new church that they were starting. It was by attending this church together that we really got to know each other. We were both single and we both had the uncanny timing of showing up in the parking lot at the same time every Sunday. We would walk in together and sit together. People who didn't know us thought we were a married couple. We laughed about it because we never held hands or acted romantic around each other. They claimed that was the basis for their marriage assessment. If we were dating, then we would have been more intimate together, so the lack of physical touch caused them to assume we must be married! It's really sad because if you look around at couples you know, there's a lot of truth behind it.

Once we were married, I started meeting with a small group of newlywed women on a weekly basis. We met together for a few years, until someone moved, someone else got a new job and life took us different directions. It was from this group that I started to set spiritual goals for myself.

The spiritual goals I set included things such as daily praying for my kids, joining the Moms In Touch group in my neighborhood and other areas of ministry I want to get involved in. In 2001, I purchased a one year bible and set a goal to read the entire book. In 2005, I participated in different bible studies and bought Michael a new bible personalized with his name. A lot of my goals are baby steps to bigger things. One year, I decided to join our Mothers of Preschoolers (MOPs) group and I ended up as the Coordinator of the group for two years. I still see the rewards of that decision in things I'm involved with today.

I try to break my goals down into manageable chunks, ideally, just out of my current comfort zone. I want to be stretched a little bit, enough to see personal improvement, but not so much that I'll give up before I start.

Home Improvement Goals

The home improvement goals often include a large do-it-yourself project we want to tackle. This is always changing. As homeowners, there is always something that has to get done. Sometimes, I feel as if our home truly is a money pit.

There was a year where I wanted to "Clean Sweep" each room of the house, focusing on one area of the house per month. I could easily divide my house into twelve categories and I took on the idea of ruthless purging. We did this after I read Peter Walsh's book, *It's All Too Much*. We trashed, we gave away and we held the mother of all garage sales. Our friends and family donated their unwanted items to the garage sale and it was my mom who contributed the most. She's quite the cheerleader for us. We used the money we made selling our extra stuff to help fund part of our trip to Europe. I wrote Peter's editor a note about. I was so excited to see the name 'Harpo Studios' (Oprah Winfrey's company) on my caller ID. They asked us to share our story on Peter Walsh's radio show. (Peter Walsh is a regular on the Oprah Winfrey Show.) I kept erasing all the other phone numbers from the caller ID so I could be reminded that Oprah's people had called me!

In 2002, we worked on the second phase of our backyard that included building a new deck and in 2004 we replaced the kitchen linoleum with a heated tile floor. This year, we need to have the exterior of our house painted. We've already secured a proposal and are set to go, just as soon as I decide on colors. I don't think I've written that on my what-to-do list, so there's no wonder why I haven't done it.

Before we were homeowners, this category included saving for our first home and researching areas we wanted to live in, choosing the school districts and discovering financing options. Our goals are not always pure fun and delight, but they are baby steps that move us forward.

Room of the Month "Clean Sweep" List

Each month, I would choose one room or area of the house to "Clean Sweep". I would ruthlessly purge all my un-wanted, un-needed or un-desired items into three categories: Trash, Donate, and Sell. Only the most treasured items that I still used got to stay and were put back in a neat and organized fashion.

January	Master Bedroom & Closet
February	Home Office & Tax Preparation
March	Bathrooms & Laundry Room
April	Kitchen
May	Garage & Prep for Garage Sale
June	Outdoor Living Space & Yard
July	Living Room & Entertainment Center
August	Children's Bedrooms & Closets
September	Basement & Storage Areas
October	Seasonal Items
November	Entry Space (where everything gets dropped when you first come home)
December	If you've covered the entire house, take the month off, otherwise, what did I miss?

Empty

By Rachel Snyder

Pour it out. Dump it out. Throw it out. Empty every bag,
box and bureau. Empty every closet, every corner, every
cupboard, every cell. Pull it out. Drag it out. Clean it
out. Clear it out. Spread it out, sort it out. Look at
what you've collected, what you've stored, what
you carry around with you every day of your
life. Empty out the old, the unwanted,
the unusable. Empty out the pain, the
heartache, the memories. Empty
everything that offers nothing.
Leave things empty for a
while. Feel empty. Feel the
lack. Feel your way
through the
nothingness,
until at last
you feel
ready to
fill.

Family Goals

Our family goals haven't seen too many changes over the years. We mostly focus on spending more family time together with activities such as sitting down together at the dinner table every night, limiting television on school nights and vacations we want to splurge on. We love to take vacations. We can be pretty frugal about most things, but vacationing is our hot button. We rarely go out to dinner, we are still using my parent's hand-me-down sofas in the living room and we have a garage-sale find for the kitchen table. However, as a family, we have been to twenty-seven different states, including Hawaii and five countries: Canada, France (twice), Spain, Italy and London.

When I met Jay, he carried around his passport as a second form of identification. He had never used it to travel outside the United States, but he wanted to. We dreamed a lot about traveling. My family traveled all throughout my childhood years. A lot of our trips were scheduled around being relocated with the Navy. My parents would send our belongings ahead of us and we would take extra time to sightsee and visit friends and family. So many of my childhood memories take place in my dad's Chevy pickup truck with the custom camper shell that we slept in. Still today, we can be out late at night and I'll have a memory flashback to where I'm sitting right next to my dad as he drove through the night, while my brother, sister and mom were asleep in the back of the truck. As a little girl, I don't ever remember my dad sleeping. We would go on these long road trips and my dad would just drive forever. He would have his country music on and be thumping the steering wheel with his thumb and I would watch the big eighteen wheeler truckers go by. My dad had a CB and trucker name and he would talk to other people about traffic or speed traps or stuff I didn't understand because it was like listening to a foreign language. I'm sure those road trips helped instill my love for traveling.

Personal Goals

Writing this book is a personal goal for me. For a long time, I've wanted to be an author. It's my dream professional title. And not just one book, but I want to write several. Jay tells me that once I make it as an author, I can have a "writing house". My "writing house" would be free of distractions like the telephone and the doorbell and having to stop for anything while my fingers fly across the keyboard. My "writing house" would be full of brainstorming qualities like never-ending cups of hot tea, a fireplace, an inspiring view of the ocean and stacks of books for reading.

I would love to eat a healthy, clean diet and exercise every day for a little while. I would love to drink more water and make healthier lifestyle choices.

I would love to speak French, fluently. I took four years of French in high school, two years in middle school and two years in college. I've been to Paris three times. You would think I would be fluent in the universal language of love, but, non! However, I still remember how to conjugate my verbs: Je parle, tu parle, vous parlez, nous parlons!

As soon as Parisians discover that I'm an American, they practice speaking to me in English, so I've yet to find the crowd that speaks French in my little suburban world. Though, I recently joined a French-speaking group on Meetup.com, so I can check that off as another step towards that personal goal.

Financial Goals

The fact of the matter is that most of my dreams also include having to set a simultaneous financial goal, too. They seem to go together like peanut butter and jelly.

I have read and re-read Dave Ramsey's *Financial Peace* book and the answer to financial peace is always the same; spend less, save more. In our home, we try to spend less than we make. If we can't afford to pay for the entire purchase, then we wait and save some more.

For several years, our only financial goal was "No More Debt". This was harder than we thought. We had gotten ourselves so used to spending on our credit cards, or applying for car loans, that we didn't even realize how detrimental we were being towards our own financial health. I once heard a motivational speaker say that he was debt-free and drama-free and the audience chuckled. I thought, now there's a fairy tale we can all dream for.

Setting goals doesn't have to be complicated, in fact; we try to keep it really simple. We were given a dream book from our financial planner and it made dreaming really fun and easy. Not every dream is a big pipe dream. Sometimes the dream is really attainable, especially once you write it down and make a decision to accomplish it. Sometimes, I'll have to re-write a goal. For example, one year, Jay and I decided we wanted to take dance lessons. Okay, *I* decided that *we* wanted to learn to dance together. We didn't do it. Then the next year, we wrote it down again. It got to be October and the year was quickly coming to an end. We found classes though the community center and finally signed up for the lessons. We had so much fun learning to dance together. We ended up continuing to take lessons for over a year - and we wouldn't have done it if we hadn't written it down on our dream list.

I recommend that you clear some space in your calendar and invite a loved one to join you in making a dream list. Often, we can talk ourselves in and out of a dream in the blink of an eye, so it's fun to have someone to spur you on and then later hold you accountable. You get to hold them accountable, too, so it's fair game. If you let yourself relax and really get into it, this can be really fun. You might discover a spark that just needed a little fuel.

To get the brainstorming juices flowing, make a list of one hundred dreams. Ask yourself "What if?" What if you could? What if there weren't any excuses? What if it all fell in your lap? You'll start with places you want to go, personal and professional goals, qualities to develop, habits to change. As you rattle off those dreams on the top of your head, you'll have to think a little harder, go back to your youth a little bit and listen to your spirit reminding you of those dreams you gave up long ago. Do you want to spend more time with your family? Go back to school? Volunteer? Start a business, travel? What legacy do you want to leave behind?

- From the list, pick two or three dreams that you want to achieve in the next twelve months.

- Be as specific as you can about what it means to achieve that dream.

- Set a date or a timeline to accomplish the dream.

- Guess at how much it will cost. You can do some research and fill this in more accurately, later.

- List the action steps it requires. For example, if you're planning a trip, you might need to talk to a travel agent about the itinerary and costs, determine your budget, schedule time off from work and create a plan for how you will save up for it.

- If you're worried about getting derailed, find a picture that represents your dream and put it someplace you'll see every day. It helps to remind yourself why you're working so hard or sacrificing to make that dream come true. Is it a dream destination that you've always wished for? Does it hold a special memory? Is it an opportunity you will regret not doing? Put up reminders.

I hope you envision the possibilities for your future.

Here is the Bucket List that was sent to me on Facebook. It's a list of one hundred dreams. The instructions were to put an X next to all the things you had done and leave it blank if you hadn't. At the end, add your own item of something you've done.

(X) Been to Canada
(X) Been to Florida
(X) Been to Hawaii
(X) Been on an airplane
(X) Been on a helicopter
(X) Been lost
(X) Gone to Washington, DC
(X) Swam in the ocean
(X) Consoled someone who was crying
(X) Played cops and robbers
(X) Recently colored with crayons
(X) Sang karaoke
(X) Paid for a meal with coins only
( ) Paid off the house
(X) Been to the top of the St. Louis Arch
(X) Done something you told yourself you wouldn't
(X) Made prank phone calls
( ) Been down Bourbon Street in New Orleans
(X) Laughed until some kind of beverage came out of your nose
(X) Caught a snowflake on your tongue
( ) Danced in the rain-naked
(X) Written a letter to Santa Claus
(X) Been kissed under the mistletoe
(X) Watched the sunrise with someone
(X) Blown bubbles
(X) Gone ice-skating
(X) Gone to the movies

( ) Been deep sea fishing
(X) Driven across the United States
( ) Been in a hot air balloon
( ) Been sky diving
( ) Gone snowmobiling
(X) Lived in more than one country
(X) Lay down outside at night and admired the stars while listening to the crickets
(X) Seen a falling star and made a wish
(X) Enjoyed the beauty of Old Faithful Geyser
(X) Seen the Statue of Liberty
(X) Gone to the top of Seattle Space Needle
( ) Been on a cruise
(X) Traveled by train
( ) Traveled by motorcycle
(X) Been horse back riding
(X) Ridden on a San Francisco cable car
(X) Been to Disneyland --- or Disney World
( ) Been in a rain forest
(X) Seen whales in the ocean
( ) Been to Niagara Falls
( ) Ridden on an elephant
( ) Swam with dolphins
( ) Been to the Olympics
( ) Walked on the Great Wall of China
( ) Saw and heard a glacier calve
( ) Been spinnaker flying
(X) Been water-skiing
(X) Been snow-skiing
(X) Been to Westminster Abbey
(X) Been to the Louvre
(X) Swam in the Mediterranean
(X) Been to a Major League Baseball game
( ) Been to a National Football League game

94

(X) Thrown up after riding a roller coaster or other carnival ride
(X) Buried a pet
( ) Auditioned for a television show
(X) Peed in the woods
( ) Visited the Taj Mahal
( ) Been to Iran
(X) Walked on the bridge at Royal Gorge
(X) Stood up for yourself
( ) Been to a National Hockey League game
( ) Been to Jamaica
( ) Won a school spelling bee
( ) Was an extra in a movie
( ) Hit a 'hole in one' in golf (i.e. not miniature)
( ) Spoke with someone over 100 years old
( ) Been to all 50 states
(X) Been to the top of the Empire State Building
( ) Delivered a baby animal
(X) Fallen asleep in the arms of someone you love
( ) Been to a World Series Game (Does not apply to Cub Fans)
(X) Been to a High School Football State Championship Game
(X) Wet your pants
(X) Lied to your mother
( ) Rode the NYC Subway
( ) Been to Africa
( ) Ridden a gondola in Venice
(X) Saw the Vegas lights from above
( ) Been to the Alps
( ) Bungee jumped off a bridge
( ) Nursed a wounded animal back to health
(X) Learned to drive a manual transmission
(X) Taken the English Tunnel to United Kingdom from France
( ) Seen the Egyptian Pyramids
(X) Laughed so hard you cried

(X) Had a car accident and nobody was in the car
(X) Had emergency surgery
( ) Parasailed
( ) Zip-lined through the trees
(X) Taken a car-ferry across Lake Michigan
(X) Paid for the orthodontist with $1 bills

CHAPTER ELEVEN
The Recommended Reading List

You don't have to burn books to destroy a culture; just get people to stop reading them. – Ray Bradbury

This is a list of books that I use for referencing all the time. I always have a stack of books on my nightstand and I am a regular user of my public library, but these are the books that I keep bookmarks in and refer back to the most.

My friends are always sending me reading recommendations, so I had to start keeping a list of the books I want to read. I've included a blank check list for you in the back of this book.

Total Money Makeover
Dave Ramsey

There's no quick-fix to becoming debt-free. Most of us didn't get there quickly and most of us won't get out quickly, but we can change our habits and Dave Ramsey teaches you how to do it in seven baby steps.

98
You and Your Child
Charles Swindoll

Before my daughters could walk, I read *You and Your Child*. I kept it close at hand as they hit milestone after milestone. We still reach for the book when we are having long discussions with the kids.

The One-Minute Mother
Spencer Johnson, MD

When I first saw that a man had written the One-Minute Mother, I thought to myself, how absurd! And then I found myself in the pages. My children didn't need long lectures or drawn out discipline from me, they needed me to decisive and loving and I found great tips in the One-Minute Mother.

Basic Black
Cathie Black

Cathie Black is the President of Hearst Magazines and the woman who persuaded Oprah Winfrey to launch her own magazine. I love Cathie's helpful and down-to-earth advice. Her personal stories show you that there are opportunities all around, even in our mistakes.

It's All Too Much
Peter Walsh

This book inspired me to clear the clutter out of my house. It not only freed me from my overabundance of stuff, but it also released me from the constant activity of putting things away and keeping after the kids to clean up. Plus, we took the money we earned by selling off our extra stuff to partially fund our European vacation.

The Yearly Bible

It's easy to commit to reading the bible on a daily basis when it's broken down into manageable sections. I didn't read it in full the first year I bought it and I've only done it once in all these years. Sometimes, I'll just flip it open to the current date and be amazed at how comforting and specific the words are in that moment.

Entre Nous – A Woman's Guide to Finding Her Inner French Girl
Debra Ollivier

Sometimes, I imagine that I am a French girl trapped inside an American body. It's a very romantic notion. I dream of the simplicity of the French girl's closet and I reference this book often when I'm clearing out or shopping for new.

The Dream Book
Ameriprise.com

This is a workbook that my financial advisor handed me when I first retained him. Filling out this book has kept our financial goals on track. We didn't start planning for retirement until after Jay turned forty, but even with the stock market slump, we are still hitting our financial goals.

The Sonoma Diet
Dr. Connie Gutterson

The list of the ten perfect foods came from this book. I don't spend a lot of time in the kitchen and many of the recipes in this book have way too many ingredients for me, but I like the idea of eating foods high in nutrients, flavor and color. It also includes an effective ten-day diet.

Detoxify Your Lifestyle
Dr. Nick Caras

For a simple and easy-to-follow guide on developing healthy lifestyle habits, Dr. Nick's checklists and quizzes are a great reference tool.

CHAPTER TWELVE
Wrap It Up

All you need is love. – The Beatles

My parents are planning to retire in a few years and move out of state. It will be the furthest away from them that I've ever known. My dad traveled quite a bit with his naval career, but it was always temporary. They've decided that they want to enjoy their retirement years in fun retirement community and despite my suggestions of staying in the local area; they say that there isn't any place in Denver that suits their needs. Part of me thinks that my parents won't last more than a few years being away from all their grandchildren and I'm sure they'll decide that they miss me and they'll want to move back in a few years! My mom has always been my biggest cheerleader and I'll miss not having her here.

I am excited for them, though. They have a dream that they are looking forward to and it's exciting for them to talk about. Even though it's still a few years away, my mom is actively planning what to take and what to bequeath to her children. Knowing my mom, she'll plan some type of ceremony, complete with costumes, where we all show up and receive our packages and say good-bye to the house they live in now. She might even have her belongings all gift-wrapped for us. I love receiving gift-wrapped presents!

When I was pregnant with my twin daughters, I spent a lot of time in the hospital with complications. My mom would visit me everyday. Most days she would arrive with a shopping bag full of wonderful baby items to cheer me up. She would glide into the room with something perky to say and flash me her fabulous smile.

She would say, "I brought you a present!"

But the gifts weren't wrapped up in wrapping paper or tissue paper or anything. They were just purchases in a shopping bag. That was when I discovered that I love to receive gift-wrapped gifts. If you call it a present, I think it should be wrapped up like one. You've seen toddlers who are more amused by the box that the toy comes in, than the toy itself. That's me. I am into the packaging. There is something special about a wrapped gift. I get all caught up in the colorful paper, the curly ribbons and crumpled up tissue paper. It doesn't matter what you wrap up, the gift-wrapping makes the gift very special to me. Now, my mom brings me the most embellished-wrapped gifts. It's fantastic.

I once took a part-time job working in an office supply store that also provided gift-wrapping services. We had a shipping counter and our customers often came in with presents they were mailing off to loved ones. I learned how to gift-wrap when I worked here. Until then, I underestimated the power of curling ribbon on a package. It's now one of my favorite embellishments. You can put curling ribbon on a brown paper bag and all of a sudden it has mass appeal.

At the end of the day, all of my lists aren't all that exciting. Making lists isn't the thing that motivates me to get out of bed, even though my 'Oh, Shoot!' pad gets a lot of use when I first wake up in the morning. My lists are the wrapping paper to my dreams. Without the lists to remind me to move forward and to take care of the details, I wouldn't be able to wrap my dreams up with a pretty bow. Checklists are like curling ribbon that keeps my teeter-totter life all wrapped up.

I'm so blessed to have a family that dreams. I'm blessed to have teenager daughters who still talk to me and hug me and tell me "Happy Wednesday". They are as optimistic as the day is long. I am blessed to have a pre-teen son who still lets me walk him to and from school. I am blessed to be married to my own James Bond. I am blessed to have a business partner who encourages me to spend time with my family. All around me are people who love me and people who support me. If everything else fails, I am still a success because of those who love me.

104

APPENDIX

The Appendix is there for a reason... right? – Unknown

The Calendar

The What-To-Do List

The Chore List

The Honey-Do List

The Room-of-the-Month List

The Money List

The Ultimate Packing List

The Shopping List

The Menu

The Special Date List

The Dream List

The Reading List

The Bucket List

THE CALENDAR

The calendar is the ultimate "to-do" list. I keep one master calendar for both personal and professional appointments, including my children's activities. Keeping it all in one place keeps me from double booking and from missing out on important meetings.

THE CALENDAR

Sunday	Monday	Tuesday	Wednesday	Thursday	Friday	Saturday

THE WHAT-TO-DO LIST

Each week, I create a brand new list of what needs to be done. After reviewing last week's list, I can determine what items need to be delegated or moved to the top of the list. I check off the items once they're finished rather that crossing items off the list. This technique makes it easy to back and read through my lists and keeps the pages looking cleaner.

THE WHAT-TO-DO LIST

*Date*_____

THE CHORE LIST

Each child gets their own chore list, based on age-appropriate chores. I change their chore list every three months or so to keep it interesting. Plus, they tend to slack off on their quality if they have the same chore list for too long. In the beginning, I had to remind them often to do their chores, but once the habits set in, my role was minimized. That's when the chore list reaped its value.

THE CHORE LIST

Monday	Tuesday	Wednesday	Thursday	Friday

THE HONEY-DO LIST

The Honey-Do list is both a blessing and a curse, and depending on the project, it can vary. Most items on the list could be completed without turning into an additional project, but not always. I keep my honey-do list to a maximum of five items at any given time and always give a deadline. Having company over is a great deadline!

THE HONEY-DO LIST

Request	Due Date

THE ROOM-OF-THE-MONTH LIST

By focusing on one area of my house to clean out each month, I feel like the overwhelming project of keeping my home organized is manageable. It takes this monstrous task and breaks it down to something that can be accomplished in an afternoon, or at most, a weekend. I keep thinking that I'll get a handle on the influx of items that continuously flow into my home, and this task will go away, but I haven't mastered that one yet. I'm still looking for more ways to cut out what comes in. Until then, I tackle one area of my house each month.

THE ROOM-OF-THE-MONTH LIST

January	
February	
March	
April	
May	
June	
July	
August	
September	
October	
November	
December	

THE MONEY LIST

Rather than get to the end of the month or the year and wonder, "where did all my money go?", I assign my dollars a name and a place. It's easier to set goals, manage money and make productive decisions. "I want it" or "I deserve it" are not productive decisions. If you want it, add it to the money list, and figure out from where you'll pull the money to pay for it.

Without a budget, I find myself reacting emotionally to our financial situation. With a budget, this stress is eliminated. I don't have to be the bad guy. I don't have to blame or make excuses. I am accountable to my budget and my budget is accountable to me.

THE MONEY LIST

Amount	Category

THE ULTIMATE PACKING LIST

It's amazing how much we can do without while traveling. I used to try to imagine every possible scenario and pack for it accordingly, only to curse myself for my foolishness later. Keeping it simple makes life so much easier both in preparing for the trip and while actually traveling.

THE ULTIMATE PACKING LIST

	Travel Wear
	Lounge Outfit/Sleepwear
	Pool Wear
	Sightseeing Wear

THE SHOPPING LIST

Using a shopping list reduces impulse purchases and keeps me focused. It also helps the rest of my family plan ahead so the task doesn't fall completely on my shoulders.

THE SHOPPING LIST

THE MENU

I create a menu at the start of each week and plan my grocery shopping for only what I need. I keep the menu on the front of my refrigerator and everyone can see what's coming up.

THE MENU

Sunday	Monday	Tuesday	Wednesday	Thursday	Friday	Saturday

Sunday	Monday	Tuesday	Wednesday	Thursday	Friday	Saturday

THE SPECIAL DATE LIST

Sending out cards for special occasions is such a treat because it hardly ever happens. Most of the mail we receive is junk or bills. Instead of sending electronic cards or e-wishes, I love to fill mailboxes with handwritten note cards.

THE SPECIAL DATE LIST

January	February	March

April	May	June

July	August	September

October	November	December

THE DREAM LIST

I've been dreaming since my childhood and just because I've grown up doesn't mean I should stop. I search my soul for that long lost dream, or sometimes I find it in a fortune cookie. I write my dreams down and I refer to them often.

THE DREAM LIST

Done	Spiritual
	Home Improvement
	Family
	Personal
	Financial

THE READING LIST

I love to read and I especially love reading books that others have recommended to me. It gives us something to connect over. I keep a list of books that I would like to read and it's fascinating to look back at the list and see my reading habit develop into fifteen books in a year.

THE READING LIST

Read	Book Title

THE BUCKET LIST

I didn't create this bucket list – it was sent to me via Facebook. The bucket list is an alternate dream list. Check off all of those items you've accomplished, add something to it that you'd like to do and then share it with others.

RE-CREATED BUCKET LIST

( ) Been to Canada
( ) Been to Florida
( ) Been to Hawaii
( ) Been on an airplane
( ) Been on a helicopter
( ) Been lost
( ) Gone to Washington, DC
( ) Swam in the ocean
( ) Consoled someone who was crying
( ) Played cops and robbers
( ) Recently colored with crayons
( ) Sang karaoke
( ) Paid for a meal with coins only
( ) Paid off the house
( ) Been to the top of the St. Louis Arch
( ) Done something you told yourself you wouldn't
( ) Made prank phone calls
( ) Been down Bourbon Street in New Orleans
( ) Laughed until some kind of beverage came out of your nose
( ) Caught a snowflake on your tongue
( ) Danced in the rain-naked
( ) Written a letter to Santa Claus
( ) Been kissed under the mistletoe
( ) Watched the sunrise with someone
( ) Blown bubbles
( ) Gone ice-skating
( ) Gone to the movies
( ) Been deep sea fishing
( ) Driven across the United States
( ) Been in a hot air balloon
( ) Been sky diving
( ) Gone snowmobiling

132

( ) Lived in more than one country
( ) Lay down outside at night and admired the stars while listening to the crickets
( ) Seen a falling star and made a wish
( ) Enjoyed the beauty of Old Faithful Geyser
( ) Seen the Statue of Liberty
( ) Gone to the top of Seattle Space Needle
( ) Been on a cruise
( ) Traveled by train
( ) Traveled by motorcycle
( ) Been horse back riding
( ) Ridden on a San Francisco cable car
( ) Been to Disneyland --- or Disney World
( ) Been in a rain forest
( ) Seen whales in the ocean
( ) Been to Niagara Falls
( ) Ridden on an elephant
( ) Swam with dolphins
( ) Been to the Olympics
( ) Walked on the Great Wall of China
( ) Saw and heard a glacier calve
( ) Been spinnaker flying
( ) Been water-skiing
( ) Been snow-skiing
( ) Been to Westminster Abbey
( ) Been to the Louvre
( ) Swam in the Mediterranean
( ) Been to a Major League Baseball game
( ) Been to a National Football League game
( ) Thrown up after riding a roller coaster or other carnival ride
( ) Buried a pet
( ) Auditioned for a television show
( ) Peed in the woods
( ) Visited the Taj Mahal

( ) Been to Iran
( ) Walked on the bridge at Royal Gorge
( ) Stood up for yourself
( ) Been to a National Hockey League game
( ) Been to Jamaica
( ) Won a school spelling bee
( ) Was an extra in a movie
( ) Hit a 'hole in one' in golf (i.e. not miniature)
( ) Spoke with someone over 100 years old
( ) Been to all 50 states
( ) Been to the top of the Empire State Building
( ) Delivered a baby animal
( ) Fallen asleep in the arms of someone you love
( ) Been to a World Series Game (Does not apply to Cub Fans)
( ) Been to a High School Football State Championship Game
( ) Wet your pants
( ) Lied to your mother
( ) Rode the NYC Subway
( ) Been to Africa
( ) Ridden a gondola in Venice
( ) Saw the Vegas lights from above
( ) Been to the Alps
( ) Bungee Jumped off a bridge
( ) Nursed a wounded animal back to health
( ) Learned to drive a manual transmission
( ) Taken the English Tunnel to United Kingdom from France
( ) Seen the Egyptian Pyramids
( ) Laughed so hard you cried
( ) Had a car accident and nobody was in the car
( ) Had emergency surgery
( ) Parasailed
( ) Zip-lined through the trees

ABOUT THE AUTHOR

Angel Tuccy considers herself to be an entrepreneurial muse who loves to write, read and travel with her family. She is the founder of *Experience Pros University*, the co-author of the book *Leading The Revolution* and the host of a daily radio show in Denver, Colorado.

Find out more at www.ExperiencePros.com.

For sixteen years, she has successfully juggled the roles of working mom and business owner. She speaks each month at the South Metro Denver Chamber of Commerce and runs a professional women's support group called *Ladies Who Lunch*. She is also on the Board of Directors for the Chamber of Commerce of Highlands Ranch, Colorado.

Angel and her husband, Jay are the parents of three children. They live in Highlands Ranch, Colorado.

Look for her children's book, *Mommy Has Lots To Do*, coming out soon.

136

Made in the USA
Lexington, KY
11 February 2012